The Fruit

Published to coincide with ~~a~~ ~~~~ ~~~~ ~~action
starting Ralph Richardson, ~~~~ *~~~~ of Enlightenment* is a
remarkable rediscovery. At first glance it seems Chekhovian with
its gently satirical portrait of a bored and fractious upper-class
Moscow family caught up in an obsession with seances and
spiritualism, yet Tolstoy wrote this comedy some years before
Chekhov's first major play. What makes the play Tolstoy's own
is his dignified treatment of the peasants who come to this
decadent household wanting to buy for themselves the land they
have worked on all their lives. In the course of an extremely
lively plot, animated as in the best comic tradition by the spirited
chambermaid, Tolstoy allows us the pleasing spectacle of fools
exposed and natural justice triumphant.

The translation is by the novelist and playwright Michael Frayn,
whose translation of *The Cherry Orchard* received wide praise
when it was performed at the National Theatre in 1978. He
has also provided a full introduction to the play and a chronology
of Tolstoy's life and works.

*The portrait of Tolstoy on the back cover is by I.N. Kramskoy
and is reproduced by courtesy of the Radio Times Hulton
Picture Library.*

Methuen's Theatre Classics

The Bacchae of Euripides — *an English version by Wole Soyinka*

Lady Precious Stream — *adapted by S.I. Hsiung from a sequence of traditional Chinese plays*

Ironhand — Goethe *adapted by John Arden*

The Government Inspector — Gogol *an English version by Edward O. Marsh and Jeremy Brooks*

Woyzeck — Büchner *translated by John MacKendrick*

Danton's Death — Büchner *an English version by James Maxwell*

Brand
Hedda Gabler
The Master Builder
Ghosts
Peer Gynt
An Enemy of the People
A Doll's House
The Wild Duck — Ibsen *translated with full introductions by Michael Meyer*

The Importance of Being Earnest
Lady Windermere's Fan — Wilde

The Ubu Plays — Jarry *translated by Cyril Connolly and Simon Watson Taylor*

The Cherry Orchard — Chekhov *translated by Michael Frayn*

Enemies
The Lower Depths — Gorky *English versions by Kitty Hunter-Blair and Jeremy Brooks*

The Playboy of the Western World — Synge

The Madras House — Granville Barker

The Guardsman — Molnár *translated by Frank Marcus*

To Ann & Simon

Lev Tolstoy

THE FRUITS
OF ENLIGHTENMENT

A Comedy in Four Acts

Translated and introduced by
MICHAEL FRAYN

with love from Lord Fruits.

Enlightenment, July 1979

EYRE METHUEN
LONDON

P.T.O.

This translation first published in 1979
by Eyre Methuen Ltd,
11 New Fetter Lane, London EC4P 4EE
Translation copyright © 1979 by Michael Frayn
Introduction and chronology copyright © 1979 by Michael Frayn
Set IBM Journal by ⚑ Tek-Art, Croydon, Surrey.
Printed in Great Britain by
Cox & Wyman Ltd., Fakenham, Norfolk

ISBN 0 413 45830 X

Lord Frinks

Lev Tolstoy

1828 Born at Yasnaya Polyana, his family's comfortably wealthy estate 130 miles south of Moscow.

1831 His mother dies, leaving the children to be brought up by 'Aunt' Toinette — an adoring cousin of his father's, who becomes Lev's confidante throughout his childhood and young manhood.

1837 His father dies, and the children's grandmother and another aunt, Aline, join Aunt Toinette in keeping the family going; they engage a staff of eleven tutors to educate the children.

1841 With both their grandmother and Aunt Aline now dead, the legal guardianship of the children passes to another aunt, Pelagya, who hates Aunt Toinette, and who brutally removes the children from her custody at Yasnaya Polyana to her home in Kazan.

1844 Tolstoy enters (with difficulty) the University of Kazan. Fails in the Department of Oriental Languages, and transfers to the Department of Law, but in fact spends most of his time in social life and reading — above all Rousseau.

1847 Drops out of university and takes over his inheritance, the Yasnaya Polyana estate, with its 4,000 acres and 330 souls.

1848 Abandons his plans to reform the estate, in the face of the peasants' resistance, and departs for Moscow and St. Petersburg, where his gambling debts force him to sell off 22 of his serfs.

1849 Seduces Aunt Toinette's maid, who is consequently dismissed — one of the victims of Tolstoy's growing taste for taking servant girls and peasant women on the estate, and then giving himself up to self-loathing.

1851 Attempts to flee his dissipation by travelling to the Caucasus, the Wild West of the Russian Empire, where he enlists as a gentleman volunteer and writes his first fiction — a story published under the title *Childhood,* which achieves immediate popular and critical success.

1854 Posted to Sevastopol, where he remains throughout the

siege, combining reckless gambling at cards with courage under fire and brilliant war-reporting.

1855 Arrives in St Petersburg as a hero, comes into contact for the first time with the literary world, and quarrels with everyone in it -- Turgenyev most resoundingly, repeatedly, and woundingly of all.

1856 Returns to Yasnaya Polyana with projects for selling his peasants the land they work, but gives up, raging, in the face of their obstinacy and suspicion.

1860 Makes the second of two journeys to Western Europe, which leave him disgusted with European materialism.

1861 Appointed local arbiter under the Emancipation Act to settle disputes arising about land between landowners and their liberated serfs. Earns the resentment of both sides, and after ten months resigns. Opens fourteen schools for the peasant children of the district, run on deschooling lines, under the motto 'Do as you like!', but loses interest in them.

1862 Marries Sonya Behrs, aged 18, insisting first that she reads his private diaries, which detail all his brutal and contempt-uous relations with women up to then. Reading each other's woundingly frank diaries becomes a regular and complicating feature of their increasingly difficult marriage.

1864 Begins *War and Peace,* and works on it for the next five years, with Sonya both serving as one of the models for Natasha Rostova and copying out most of the manuscript seven times.

1873 Begins *Anna Karenina,* and works on it for the next four years, distracted by a renewed interest in educating his peasants.

1879 Writes his *Confession,* in which he records his conversion to a form of non-metaphysical, non-ecclesiastical Christianity involving the renunciation of violence and property.

1881 Moves to a huge town house in Moscow, from which he makes excursions into the slums to study the poor, while Sonya establishes her weekly 'at home' day.

1883 Meets Chertkov, who becomes his disciple, and who begins
to organise Tolstoyism as a sect with a rigidly maintained
body of doctrine.

1886 Write his first effective play, *The Power of Darkness,* and
begins *The Fruits of Enlightenment.*

1889 Celebrates 27 years of marriage by making Sonya the model
for the wife in *The Kreutzer Sonata,* a rhapsody on the
loathsomeness of women and of sexual relations even
within marriage. Completes *The Fruits of Enlightenment;*
commences *Resurrection.*

1901 Excommunicated for his attacks on the church, although
by this time he is venerated throughout the world as the
seer of the age.

1910 Flees from home in the middle of the night, to escape the
endless warfare between his followers and his deeply
estranged wife and family. Heads south, but falls ill aboard
the train, is taken in by a wayside stationmaster at Astapovo,
and dies in the stationmaster's house a week later, besieged
by the world's press.

Introduction

Tolstoy is probably better known in England for the boots he
insisted on making, in one of his phases of social and spiritual
self-mortification, than for his plays. But the drama was a form to
which he returned over and over again during his career. He
tended to see plays as vehicles for his didactic aspirations, and,
it has to be said, most of them sank under their cargoes.

He was first taken by the theatre when he arrived in St.
Petersburg in 1855 at the age of 27, the young war correspond-
ent hero of Sevastopol. He sketched out two plays with a theme
already foreshadowing *The Fruits of Enlightenment* — the
dissipation of upper-class life. One play was to show the form it
took on the country estates of the rich, and the other in their
town houses. But he was unable to decide which it was that
needed exposing the more urgently, and neither piece was
ever written. It was in the early sixties, just before he started
work on *War and Peace,* that he completed his first play — *The
Contaminated Family*, and its subject was the great historical
watershed that Russia had just crossed in 1861, the emancipation
of the serfs. The old serf-owner and his family of the title are
'contaminated' by contact with one of the New Men of the age —
in the first draft a *déclassé* student like Bazarov in Turgenyev's
Fathers and Children, in the second a money-grubbing tax official
who has learnt to conceal his greed beneath the new vocabulary
of progressive ideas. But by the time Tolstoy returned to drama
in the 1880s, with both *War and Peace* and *Anna Karenina*
behind him, his approach had changed; he had become interested
in the movement for popular theatre. It seems to have started on
one of his walks around Moscow in the early eighties, when he
saw the *balagany* on Virgin Field — simple popular farces played
in fairground booths. The audience, he wrote in his diary, were
'wretched starveling factory folk. Teach me, Lord, how to serve
them.' He decided to provide 'judicious diversion' for them by
writing *balagan* shows of his own, and started with *The First*

Distiller, a temperance tract of surprising feebleness. In the late nineties he returned to the problems of the landowning classes with an essay in dramatic autobiography, *And Light Shines in the Darkness.* The hero is a mouthpiece for Tolstoy's own disgust with the idleness of upper-class life, and his desire to give away his estate to his peasants leads him into the same kind of conflict with wife and family through which Tolstoy himself was living. It could have been a piece of intimate self-revelation, but the clumsiness of the execution makes it only too possible to imagine what a pair of Tolstoy's home-made boots looked like, and he gave up with one act still to go.

Amidst the dross, however, he wrote three plays which, in Russia at any rate, have taken their place in the repertoire as classics. The most surprising of them is perhaps the last of the three, *The Living Corpse,* which he wrote in 1900, just after *Resurrection,* when he was 72. The striking thing about it is its moral generosity. Indeed, when it appeared, posthumously, some critics found it 'anti-Tolstoyan'; some even doubted its authenticity. Its hero, Protasov, finding that his wife is in love with another man, takes to drink and low life with the Gypsies. He refuses to involve himself with the lies necessary to give his wife a divorce, but disappears from her life and conscience by faking his suicide. She is then allowed to settle down perfectly happily in a bigamous marriage with her rather stuffy admirer (who, incidentally, is called Karenin), and Protasov is allowed to enjoy a sincere and high-minded love affair with a Gypsy girl. His wife, he says, 'never had the power to creep into his soul, like Masha . . . There was no sparkle . . . there was no play in our life.' When the possibility of divorce is being considered, and the upright Karenin is asked how he can contemplate it, given his belief in the inviolability of marriage, he replies: 'Are we really all so infallible that we cannot diverge in our convictions, when life is so complicated?' When life is so complicated! As in *Anna Karenina,* the rigid moral intention slackens, and Tolstoy becomes absorbed in the richness of what is, instead of in the simplicity of what ought to be. But once again (or so it seems to me) the execution is inadequate to the material. The play is stiff and schematic, and the flesh hangs thin upon the bone.

The two best plays are undoubtedly *The Power of Darkness* and *The Fruits of Enlightenment*. They to some extent form a complementary pair — both about the condition of the peasants, and both started in the same exercise book in the same ink, almost certainly about the same time, in 1886. The late eighties were a difficult time in the Tolstoy household. His two great masterpieces of fiction had been written, and his immense energies were free to be unleashed upon an unworthy world direct. He had undergone his celebrated conversion to Christianity, or at any rate to his own reading of it, which, eschewing all metaphysical and liturgical aspects of the faith, left him free to concentrate upon the most socially disruptive and generally uncomfortable of Christ's ethical teachings. His disciple Chertkov, the high priest of the new priestless sect, was busy solidifying Tolstoy's ideas into a rigid canon, to which he would sometimes recall even the master himself. And Tolstoy had become hugely famous. He might refuse to wash, he might insist upon making boots for his servants and working alongside the peasants in the fields, but Yasnaya Polyana was more and more like the court of some mediaeval monarch. 'It is most curious to see Lev Nikolayevich among his Tolstoyans,' wrote Maxim Gorky, after spending a day at the house. 'He is like a great steeple whose bell is heard throughout the world, and all around him scurry contemptible, cringing little curs who try to bark in turn, casting anxious, jealous glances at each other to see who yapped the best, and who has made the best impression on the master.' The only ones at Yasnaya Polyana who failed to yap to the Tolstoyan tune were his family. His relations with his wife, in particular, were becoming hellish. She was jealous of the influence of his disciples, saddened by the waste of his creative abilities, often simply nauseated by the stench of him, and certainly disgusted by his sexual hypocrisy. Because these were the years obscenely summed up at the end of the decade in *The Kreutzer Sonata,* with its disgusted condemnation of all sexual relations, including those between husband and wife. And yet he could not keep away from her — she was pregnant with their thirteenth child even while he was planning the book. He wallowed in self-loathing. 'Impenitent old Narcissus,' says Henri Troyat, in his sardonically

sympathetic biography, 'eternally preoccupied with himself,
he blew on his image in the water for the sheer pleasure of seeing
it come back again when the ripples died away.'

This was the background against which the two plays were
written. *The Power of Darkness* was the positive result of
Tolstoy's involvement in the popular theatre movement; it was
intended for 'the people', or 'the big world', as he sometimes
called it, and its characters are all peasants. It is a horrifying story,
set in the same great darkness of the moon as Leskov's novella
A Lady Macbeth of the Mtsensk District (more familiar in
England as Shostakovich's opera *Katerina Ismailovna*) or the
Ostrovsky play, *The Storm*, that Janacek used in *Katya Kabanova*.
A woman murders her husband with a poison supplied by her
lover's mother. The lover marries her, but then turns his attentions
upon her stepdaughter, as a result of which the girl becomes
pregnant. Urged on by his wife and his mother, he murders the
baby at birth so that the girl can be married off, and then, at the
wedding, falls on his knees and publicly confesses. It was based
(like *Anna Karenina*) on an actual case, and the style is naturalistic
(the murder of the baby, slowly crushed to death beneath a board,
is as harrowing as anything in Edward Bond.) Tolstoy said that he
had 'raided his notebooks' to secure the authenticity of the
peasant dialogue. When it was finished he assembled forty
representative peasants, and his friend Stakhovich, a landowner
with a talent for acting, read the play to them. Tolstoy asked
them what they thought of it. They couldn't say; they hadn't
understood a word of it. The only reaction was from the man
who ran the buffet on Tula station, who guffawed intermittently
throughout.

The Fruits of Enlightenment also took its rise from an actual
incident — a seance (unsuccessful) that Tolstoy had sceptically
attended in Moscow at the apartment of Prince Lvov. In the
summer of 1886 Tolstoy fell off a cart while he was loading hay
for a peasant's widow, hurt his leg, and was forced to retire to
bed for a couple of months. To entertain him, the obliging
Stakhovich read him plays by Ostrovsky and Gogol. Unlike
Shakespeare and Chekhov (when the latter began to emerge as a
dramatist over a decade later), these were two playwrights whose

work Tolstoy enjoyed — particularly *The Government Inspector* — and he proved to be a more receptive audience for Stakhovich's performance than the peasants; the reading roused him to start work on the idea he had been nursing for a comedy about spiritualists.

After writing an act and a bit, however, he dropped it, and did not return to it until the spring of 1889, during a visit to his friend Prince Urusov. His diary entries record rapid progress but little pleasure in the work ('Set to, wrote the comedy badly . . . ' 'Sat down to write. Everything just as bad, though a lot of it . . . ' etc) until April 1, when there occurred a short-lived but touching change in his feelings familiar to anyone who has attempted to write comedy: 'Wrote Act Four very badly . . . In the evening read the comedy to Urusov, he laughed, and it seemed tolerable.'

He thought about the play gloomily on and off throughout the summer. Then in December his daughter Tatyana and the rest of the older children decided to get up some amateur theatricals at Yasnaya Polyana for the Christmas season, and asked Tolstoy for the comedy. He set to work to rewrite it — and continued to rewrite it as the cast — the children, their friends, members of the staff, and various neighbours — rehearsed it. Novikov, the children's tutor, who was playing Yakov, later gave a picture of strenuous family fun: 'A handful of the young people would copy out the parts with rapture in the morning, in the evening there were rehearsals — and afterwards, almost every day, Tolstoy would collect up the parts again and once more rewrite the play.' This jollity (it need hardly be said) was not reflected in Tolstoy's diary. 27 December: 'The children all went off to Tula to rehearse. Oppressed by the dishonesty of the life surrounding me . . . They are performing my play, and truly I think it is having an effect upon them, and that in the depths of their heart they are all conscience-stricken and a result bored. I am all the time ashamed of this mindless expense in the midst of destitution . . . Yesterday there was a rehearsal, a great crowd of people, everyone miserable.' Novikov's praise of the play he found 'distasteful even to recall.' Still, on the 30th of December, 1889, it was performed, though Tolstoy continued gloomily rewriting it into February, and reading it to his friends and disciples ('All vanity,' he notes on 25 January). In all he rewrote it seven or eight times.

In April the play was performed, by amateurs of aristocratic birth, at Tsarskoye Syelo, in the presence of the Tsar and Tsarina. A ridiculous situation then arose, entirely characteristic of the absurdly ambiguous relations between the Tsar's government and the unwashed but still noble landowner. The play was first passed by the theatrical censorship, but then banned by the Chief Directorate for Press Affairs. According to the Minister for Internal Affairs, Durnovo, the action was taken 'in view of the rumours in some circles alleging that the author intended in this comedy to mock the nobility.' Durnovo proposed to revoke the ban, on the grounds that there had by this time been a number of amateur productions in various places, followed by detailed accounts in the newspapers, 'from which it has not been found that society saw in it a malicious and offensive lampoon upon the nobility as a whole class.' But the Tsar disagreed, and personally forbade it as 'unsuitable for the stage,' though he passed it for amateur production.

And really the Tsar was right; a lampoon upon a whole class was what Tolstoy intended — and not only because of their readiness to believe in table-rapping. One of the effects of all that rewriting was to shift the emphasis of the play away from spiritualism and on to the relationship between landowner and peasants. This is of course one of the unchanging concerns of the later Tolstoy, and it has to be said that his treatment of it in the play is rather grindingly simplistic. These are three very cleaned-up peasants who have come to buy the land they work from their lord. Two of them are comic characters, one of them is sturdily outspoken — but all of them are very decent chaps, and a lesson in the virtues of the simple life. They make a strange contrast with the rapacious, drunken, murderous crew in *The Power of Darkness*. Or with the peasants who over the years had frustrated so many of Tolstoy's plans for reform at Yasnaya Polyana with their shifty, greedy obstinacy. 'Assembled before the steps,' he had once written, in his story of a landowner's day, 'were a woman in bloodstained rags, screaming that her father-in-law had tried to kill her; two brothers who had been quarrelling over the division of their property for two years, glaring at each other with loathing; a grizzled, unshaven old house-servant with the shaking hands of a drunkard, whom his son, the gardener, had brought to the master to be scolded; a muzhik who had run his wife out of his house because she had not done a stroke of work all spring; and the wife in question, sick and sobbing, not uttering a word, sitting there on the grass in front of the steps, holding out her swollen leg wrapped in dirty rags.'

Tolstoy's gibes at the credulity of the educated classes weigh a little heavy at times, too. His robust rejection of spiritualism is somewhat devalued by his apparently no less robust rejection of microbes. The sarcasm about piano-playing that he puts in the mouth of the cook is disingenuous; Tolstoy was moved to tears by music, and used to play piano duets with his wife. On the other hand, there are no jokes at the expense of ether theory, when it is mentioned by the Professor as essential to explain the transmission of light. In fact the idea of an ether had already been undercut by the Michelson-Morley experiment of 1887, and was to be consigned by Einstein in 1905 to the world of phlogiston and spirit apparitions. But of course Tolstoy could not know that; in physics and microbiology, at any rate, Christian humility and peasant common sense are no substitute for the educated intelligence he wishes to discredit.

Nevertheless, the play is charged with a real sense of fun, in spite of Tolstoy's gloomy disdain for it, as recorded in his diary. And, like all Tolstoy's work when the moralising ceases, it has the breath of life. A number of the characters are directly biographical. The Stout Lady was based on the wife of the poet Fet. Professor Wagner, zoologist and spiritualist, recognised a combination of himself and his late friend the chemist and spiritualist Professor Butlerov in the Professor of the play (Professor Kutlerov, as he was called in the early drafts) and wrote Tolstoy a very hurt letter. A well-known hypnotist called Feldmann brought proceedings against the actor who played Grossmann when the play was performed at the Moscow Arts Theatre. Novikov, the tutor, wrote later: 'In the play there appeared many beautifully observed characteristics of the life of the Tolstoys, the Rayevskys, the Trubetskoys, the Samarins, the

Filosofovs and other landowning families of my acquaintance . . .
The play was an animated representation of life at that time
among the higher nobility, even the surnames of the characters
were taken originally from real life . . . These characters were
played by the very people, or almost the very people, from whom
they had been copied (even the servants — Yasha, Fyodor, the
footman, the former cook — worked in the Tolstoys' house).'

In fact the play is a marvellous, perhaps unique, picture of a
great house at work, below as well as above stairs. And it is the
servants who are the most interesting characters. I suspect that
Tanya, the spirited and resourceful chambermaid, played at
Yasnaya Polyana by Tolstoy's daughter with the same name, was
drawn more from life as lived in *The Marriage of Figaro* and
elsewhere (indeed it is rather touching to see how Tolstoy, who in
fiction created his own forms, has struggled here, as he ventures
into the unfamiliar medium of comic theatre, to bend his material
to the conventions of the West European high comedy of the
18th century). But the others are originals, and they are put in
the dramatically interesting position of divided loyalty. They
cannot help identifying with the peasants from the estate, who
are their kinsfolk — and yet at the same time they cannot help
being almost proud of the profligacy of life in the master's house
in town, as they expound it to their wide-eyed country cousins.
It would be interesting to know what the staff at Yasnaya Polyana
thought of their representations. Did they write hurt letters?
Did they sue? Or were they as blank as the peasants in the face of
The Power of Darkness? Perhaps, at any rate, they managed a few
guffaws in the right places.

Michael Frayn

A Note on the Translation

Sir Arthur Pinero, in his introduction to the first English edition
of the play in 1890, remarks that its 'adaptability to stage
representation may not be very patent to English readers.' I think
this is the view that has generally been taken ever since by those
few English producers and directors who have read the earlier
translations. I can trace only one previous production in London
(at the Arts Theatre, in 1928). I hope that this fresh translation,
commissioned by the National Theatre in the teeth of received
opinion, will make it possible to glimpse what Russian audiences
have managed to see in the play all these years. It is true, however,
that Tolstoy's construction does present real difficulties in making
the play workable. I have therefore taken the liberty of changing
it, by rearranging some of the material in the second half.

   As Tolstoy wrote it, the seance occurs on the same day as
Semyon is tested as a medium, and its location is 'a small sitting-
room, where the Master's experiments usually take place.' More
worryingly, it happens in Act Three. This means that there is
apparently no plot left during the first half of Act Four, which is
set in the entrance hall as the guests come and go on the Mistress's
calling day. It is over halfway through this last act before Grigory
and Semyon erupt fighting from the pantry, and hopes revive
that there may be a little more story still to come. So I have
shifted the seance, which is after all the climax of the play, into
Act Four, and made it the Master's way of escaping the rigours
of his wife's 'day', the guests for which now arrive in Act Three.
I have located the seance in the study because we are now outside
the study door throughout Act Three, and there is a chance of
maintaining a little anticipation. I have had to add a few lines of
my own here and there to make this reorganisation fall into
place, but they are not obtrusive, and they do not advance any
views at variance with the author's own. Tolstoy himself rewrote
the play seven or eight times. I like to believe that if he had written
another eight drafts he might have hit upon my scheme of things.

I have made a number of discreet cuts, and have merged Tolstoy's Baroness in Act Two into his Countess in the second half of the play; a modern producer does not have a whole houseful of servants and idle guests at his disposal. I have been ruthless with names. Russian patronymics induce symptoms of hysterical withdrawal in English actors and audiences alike. Few characters in this text have been left with more than one name; several have been stripped of even that. (The complete names appear in Tolstoy's Notes on the Characters, for anyone who is interested.) I have expanded a number of allusions (to Wallace and Crookes, for example) to make them comprehensible to a twentieth-century audience, and I have removed the division of the acts into scenes at each entrance and exit, in the French manner, to make the text easier to read. And if I have managed to find a workable convention in English for the peasants' dialogue, I shall be forgiven in heaven for all this and more.

M.F.

Characters

This translation of The Fruits of Enlightenment *was scheduled for first performance by the National Theatre in the Olivier in February 1979, directed by Christopher Morahan.*

The family
THE MASTER, *Leonid Fyodorovich Zvezdintzev*
THE MISTRESS, *his wife*
BETSY, *their daughter*
VASILY, *their son*

The servants
FYODOR, *the valet*
GRIGORY, *the footman*
YAKOV, *the butler*
SEMYON, *the pantry-boy*
TANYA, *the chambermaid*
THE COACHMAN
THE OLD COOK
THE PRESENT COOK
THE DOORKEEPER

The guests and visitors
MARYA, *the music teacher*
THE PROFESSOR
THE DOCTOR
PETRISHCHEV, *Vasily's friend*
THE PRINCESS
THE PRINCESS'S DAUGHTER
THE COUNTESS
GROSSMANN, *the hypnotist*
THE STOUT LADY
COCO, *Betsy's admirer*
A LADY

A SILENT GENTLEMAN
SAKHATOV, *a former junior minister*
THE LEADING PEASANT
THE YOUNG PEASANT
THE OLDEST PEASANT
THE COUNTESS'S GROOM
THE SILENT GENTLEMAN'S GROOM
BOURDET'S MAN

The action of the play takes place in Moscow, at the home of the Zvezdintzevs

Tolstoy's Notes on the Characters

THE MASTER, Leonid Fyodorovich Zvezdintzev: an ex-lieutenant of Horse Guards, owner of 65,000 acres in various provinces. A fresh-complexioned man of about 60, mild, pleasant, and in the English sense a 'gentleman'. Believes in spiritualism and loves to astonish others with his tales.

THE MISTRESS, Anna Pavlovna Zvedintzeva, his wife: a stout, youthful-looking lady, preoccupied with social niceties, who despises her husband and has a blind faith in the doctor. An irritable lady.

BETSY, their daughter: a fashionable young lady of 20, with pince-nez and fast manners imitated from men. A coquette. Laughs a lot. Speaks very rapidly and very distinctly, pursing her lips like a foreigner.

VASILY LEONIDICH, their son: aged 25, a law graduate, of no fixed occupation. Member of a Bicycling Club, a Jockey Club, and a Club for the Encouragement of Interest in Borzois. A young man possessed of excellent health and indestructible self-confidence. Speaks loudly and abruptly. Either completely serious, almost melancholy, or else noisily cheerful and laughing loudly.

THE PROFESSOR, Aleksey Vladimirovich Krugosvyetlov: *a savant* of 50, with clam, agreeably self-confident manners and a slow-spoken, melodious voice to match. Likes talking. Short and dismissive with anyone who disagrees. A heavy smoker. A thin, active man.

THE DOCTOR: 40, a healthy, stout, red-faced man. Loud-voiced and bluntly-spoken. Keeps chuckling in a self-satisfied way.

MARYA KONSTANTINOVNA, the music teacher: a young lady of 20, a pupil at the Conservatory, with a fringe on her forehead, and an exaggeratedly fashionable *toilette*. Obsequious and shy.

PETRISHCHEV: 28, a language graduate in search of an occupation. Member of the same clubs as Vasily and also of a society for organising informal dances. Balding, quick in his movements and speech, and very polite.

THE PRINCESS: a fashionable lady.

THE PRINCESS'S DAUGHTER: a fashionable young lady, given to pulling faces.

THE COUNTESS: an ancient lady who moves only with difficulty, and who wears a wig and false teeth.

GROSSMANN: Jewish, dark, very active and nervous. Talks very loudly.

THE STOUT LADY, Marya Vasilyevna Tolbukhina: a very grand, wealthy, and good-natured lady, acquainted with all persons of note, past and present. Very stout. Speaks hurriedly, trying to talk everyone else down. Smokes.

COCO, Baron Klingen: a graduate of St. Petersburg University, a Gentleman of the Bedchamber, serving in an embassy. Absolutely correct in his behaviour, and as a result calm-spirited and quietly cheerful.

A LADY.

A GENTLEMAN, who does not speak.

SAKHATOV, Sergey Ivanovich: 50, a former Deputy Minister, an elegant gentleman of wide European education, occupied with nothing but interested in everything. Behaves with dignity, even with a certain severity.

FYODOR IVANICH, the valet: 60, a man both educated and with a respect for education, who makes great play with his pince-nez, and with a handkerchief which he is always slowly unfolding. Follows politics. An intelligent and good-hearted man.

GRIGORY, the footman: 28, handsome, licentious, envious, and bold.

YAKOV, the butler: 40, fussy, good-natured, living only for his interest in his family in the country.

SEMYON, the pantry-boy: 20, a healthy fresh-faced country lad, fair-haired, still beardless, calm, and smiling.

THE COACHMAN: 35, a dandy, with a moustache. Blunt and decisive.

THE OLD COOK: a man of 45, dishevelled, unshaven, bloated, sallow, and shaking, wearing a torn nankeen summer overcoat, dirty trousers, and broken-down shoes. Speaks hoarsely. Words escape from him as if through some obstruction.

THE PRESENT COOK: a talkative, discontented woman of 30.

THE DOORKEEPER: a discharged soldier.

TANYA, the chambermaid: 19, an energetic, strong, cheerful girl of rapidly changing moods. At moments of great excitement and joy she squeals.

FIRST PEASANT: 60. Was the village elder. Thinks he knows how to deal with the gentry, and loves the sound of his own voice.

SECOND PEASANT: 45. Owns his land. Blunt and upright. Doesn't waste words. Semyon's father.

THIRD PEASANT: 70. Wears bast shoes. A nervous, uneasy, hurrying man. Is shy, and drowns his shyness in conversation.

THE COUNTESS'S GROOM: an old man of the old school, with a servant's pride.

THE SILENT GENTLEMAN'S GROOM: huge, healthy, blunt.

BOURDET'S MAN: wears a long-waisted dark blue overcoat, and has a clean red face. Speaks firmly, persuasively, and clearly.

The Pronunciation of the Names

The following is an approximate practical guide. In general, all stressed a's are pronounced as in 'far' (the sound is indicated below by 'aa') and all stressed o's as in 'more' (they are written below as 'aw'). All unstressed a's and o's are thrown away and slurred. The u's are pronounced as in 'crude'; they are shown below as 'oo'. A y at the beginning of a syllable is pronounced as a consonant (ie. as in 'yellow', not as in 'sky'). Where the y is preceded by another consonant the two are pronounced together (ie. 'Fyodor' is pronounced like 'if *your* door' without the i sound, in two syllables, and not 'Fee-odor' or 'Fer-yordor' in three).

The characters:

Leo*need* Zvez-*deent*-sev
Va*seely*
*Fyaw*dor
Gree*gawry*
*Yaa*kov
Sem*yawn*
*Taa*nya
*Maar*ya
Pe-*treesh*-chev
Coco (French pronunciation)
Sa*khaa*tov
*Maar*ya Va*seely*evna

Other names occuring in the play, in alphabetical order:

Aksinya — Ak*seen*ya
Anisim — A*nees*eem
Bourdet — (French pronunciation)
Dmitry — *Dmeet*ry
Dodo — (French pronunciation)
Fedya — *Fed*ya

Fifka — *Feef*ka
Golovkin — Go*lawv*keen
Ivin — *Eev*een
Kapchich — *Kaap*chich
Kursk — Koorsk
Lukerya — Loo*ker*ya
Marya Ignatyevna — *Maar*ya Eeg*naat*yevna
Mergasov — *Mair*gasov
Mitry Chilikin — *Meet*ry Chee*leek*een
Mosolova — *Maw*solova
Natasha — Na*taash*a
Pironet — (French pronunciation)
Sadovaya — Sa*dawv*aya
Shcherbakov — Sh-cher*baak*ov
Shubin — *Shoob*een
Verochka Konshina — *Ver*ochka *Kawn*sheena
Vovo — (French pronunciation)
Voznosyenskoye — Vozno-*syen*sko-ye
Yefim Antonich — Ye*feem* An*tawn*eech
Zakhar Trifonich — Za*khaar* Tri*fawn*ich

Act One

The antechamber of a rich house in Moscow. Three doors: one leading to the street, one into the study occupied by the master of the house, and one into his son's room. A staircase leads up to the inner rooms; behind it is a passageway into the pantry.

GRIGORY, *the footman, is looking in the mirror and preening himself.*

GRIGORY. Pity about the moustache. Won't do for a footman, she says, wearing a moustache. And why not? So as they can see you're a footman. So as you don't outdo that precious son of hers in any way. Now there's someone. I can leave him standing, even without a moustache. There's plenty of them running after me. Only thing is, there's none of them I fancy like that Tanya. So she's nothing but a chambermaid. All right, but she's better than any lady. She's a darling, she is. Here she comes, too. Listen to those little heels tapping! Rrraugh!

Enter TANYA, *carrying a fur coat and boots.*

Present me humble respects to the young lady!
TANYA. What, you still gazing at yourself? Think you're beautiful, do you?
GRIGORY. What — ugly, am I?
TANYA. Not ugly. Not handsome. Just average. What are you leaving coats hanging out there for?
GRIGORY. I'll clear them away at once, madam. (*Takes the fur coat, wraps* TANYA *in it, and embraces her.*) I'm going to tell you a little secret, Tanya, my darling.
TANYA. Don't you my-darling me! And what's this thing doing hanging round me? (*Angrily breaks free.*) Leave me alone, can't you?
GRIGORY (*looks round*). Give us a kiss.
TANYA. Yes, and for that matter what are *you* doing hanging round me? I'll give you a kiss all right! (*Raises her hand to him.*)

A bell, off.

VASILY (*off*). Grigory!

TANYA. Go on, off you go. The young master's calling.

GRIGORY. He'll wait. He's only just rubbed his eyes. Listen, why don't you love me, then?

TANYA. What's all this you've got into your head about love? I don't love anyone.

GRIGORY. That's not true. You're in love with Semyon. A fine one you've picked yourself there, I must say. A great lump of a pantry-boy

TANYA. Well, whatever he's like, here's you jealous of him.

VASILY (*off*). Grigory!

GRIGORY. What's the hurry . . . ? Oh, yes, I've got a lot to be jealous about there, haven't I? Look, you've only just begun to find out a bit about the world — what do you want to get yourself tied up with someone for? Be another matter if it was me you was in love with. Tanya . . .

TANYA. I'm telling you, you won't get anything out of me!

VASILY (*off*). Grigory!

GRIGORY. Very prim and proper, aren't we?

VASILY (*off, with monotonous obstinacy, at the top of his voice*). Grigory! Grigory! Grigory!

TANYA *and* GRIGORY *laugh.*

GRIGORY. There's some that love me, anyway.

Doorbell.

TANYA. You go to him, then, and leave me be.

GRIGORY. You're a daft one, aren't you? I'll be keeping an eye on you. I'm not Semyon, you know!

TANYA. Semyon wants to get married. He doesn't want just a lot of nonsense.

TANYA *opens the front door.*

Enter the BOURDET'S MAN, *carrying a large cardboard dress-box.*

BOURDET'S MAN. Good morning.

GRIGORY. Hello. What shop's this, then?

BOURDET'S MAN. Bourdet's. It's a dress, and there's a note for the mistress.

TANYA (*takes the note*). You sit down here. I'll give it to her.

Exit TANYA *upstairs.*

Enter VASILY *from his room in shirt and slippers.*

VASILY. Grigory!

GRIGORY. Coming.

VASILY. Grigory, are you deaf?

GRIGORY. I've only this minute got here.

VASILY. Hot water and tea.

GRIGORY. They'll be bringing it directly.

VASILY. What's this, then? From Bourdet's?

BOURDET'S MAN. Yes, sir.

Exeunt VASILY *and* GRIGORY *into* VASILY's *room.*

Doorbell. TANYA *runs in from upstairs.*

TANYA. She says to wait.

BOURDET'S MAN. I am waiting.

TANYA *opens the front door. Enter* SAKHATOV.

TANYA. Beg pardon, sir, but the footman's just stepped out for a moment. May I . . . ? (*Takes his fur overcoat.*)

SAKHATOV (*sets himself to rights*). Is the master at home? Is he up?

Doorbell.

TANYA. Oh gracious, long since!

TANYA *opens the front door. Enter the* DOCTOR.

DOCTOR (*a little over-familiar*). Well, well, well! Minister! My humble respects to you, sir!

SAKHATOV (*stares at him*). You're the doctor, I believe?

DOCTOR. I thought you were in foreign parts. Here to see Zvezdintzev, are you?

SAKHATOV. I am. What are you doing here? Someone ill?

DOCTOR (*laughs*). I should say ill. But you know what it is with these ladies. Always in trouble. She sits up every night till three in the morning playing cards, and laces herself up as tight as an hour-glass. But she's a solidly-built party. She's getting on in years.

SAKHATOV. Do you come out with your diagnosis to the lady herself? I don't imagine she's pleased with it.

DOCTOR (*laughing*). What of it? It's the truth. They get up to all these tricks, and then it's disorders of the digestive organs, pressure on the liver, nerves playing up — there's no end to it. And then it's oh doctor, please put me right. Oh, they're a trial! But how about you? You're another of these spiritualist fellows, I believe?

SAKHATOV. I? No, sir, I am not another of these spiritualist fellows. I wish you good day, sir.

He turns to go, but the DOCTOR *stops him.*

DOCTOR. Now, well, I don't dismiss it completely, you know. Not when a man like the Professor takes part. You can't. A professor, known throughout Europe. There's something in it. Like to take a look at it myself. But I never have the time. Always other things on hand.

SAKHATOV. Quite, quite. Good day to you, then. (*Gives a small bow, and turns to go.*)

DOCTOR (*to* TANYA). Are we up and about, then?

TANYA. In the bedroom. Will you go up?

Exit the DOCTOR *upstairs.*
Exit SAKHATOV *into the* MASTER's *study.*
Enter FYODOR, *the valet, holding a newspaper.*

FYODOR (*to* BOURDET'S MAN). What are you doing here?

BOURDET'S MAN. From Bourdet's, with a dress and a note. They told me to wait.

FYODOR. Bourdet's, right. (*To* TANYA:) Who was that on their way in?

TANYA. Mr. Sakhatov and the doctor. They stopped and talked for a moment. All about spirituality.

FYODOR. Spiritualism.

TANYA. Did you hear — it worked last time. (*Laughs.*) There was a knocking, and things flew about.

FYODOR. How do you know?

TANYA. The young mistress said.

Enter YAKOV, *the butler, running, with a glass of tea.*

YAKOV (*to* BOURDET'S MAN). Good morning.

BOURDET'S MAN (*gloomily*). Good morning.

YAKOV *knocks on* VASILY's *door.* GRIGORY *appears.*

GRIGORY. Give it here.

YAKOV. And you haven't brought back the glasses from yesterday, no, nor Mr. Vasily's tray, neither. They'll be asking me for them, you know.

GRIGORY. The tray's being used. It's got his cigars on it.

YAKOV. You move them, then. They're holding me responsible.

GRIGORY. I'll bring it, I'll bring it!

YAKOV. 'I'll bring it,' you say, and where is it? They've just realised it's not there, and there's nothing to serve on.

GRIGORY. I'll bring it, I tell you! Fuss, fuss!

YAKOV. It's all very well for you to talk, but here am I, I'm serving my third tea and I'm laying up for lunch. I don't know. You wear yourself to a rag, day in, day out. Is there anyone in the house who's got more to do than me? But still, whatever I do it's wrong!

GRIGORY. Oh, come on, where would they find anyone better than you? Look at him — look what a dab hand he is!

TANYA. No one's any good according to you, are they? Only yourself.

GRIGORY. No one asked your opinion.

Exit GRIGORY *into* VASILY's *room.*

YAKOV. What's it matter, my dear? I don't take offence. I suppose the mistress hasn't said anything about that business yesterday?

TANYA. You mean about the lamp?

YAKOV. How it got away from my hands like that God knows. I was just starting to clean it. I went to pick it up, and it kind

of slipped away. And there it was in little pieces! Just my luck.
It's all right for him to talk! Grigory there — there's only one
of him. But how about when you're a family? You've got to
think about them, too, and feeding them. I can't keep my
mind on the work. So she hasn't said anything? Well, thank
God for that. And the teaspoons you've got in your room,
Fyodor — is it one or is it two?

FYODOR. One, one. (*Reads the paper.*)

> *Exit YAKOV into the pantry.*
> *Doorbell.*
> TANYA *opens the front door. Enter the* DOORKEEPER.
> *Enter* GRIGORY *from* VASILY'*s room with the tray.*

DOORKEEPER (*to* GRIGORY). Tell the master, the peasants
have arrived from the estate.

GRIGORY (*pointing to* FYODOR). Tell him. I'm busy.

> *Exit* GRIGORY *into the pantry.*

TANYA. Which estate?

DOORKEEPER. The one near Kursk, apparently.

TANYA (*squeals*). It's them! It's Semyon's father about the land!
I'm going to say hello to them.

> TANYA *runs out through the front door.*

DOORKEEPER. So what do you say — shall I let them in here or
not? They say, 'It's about the land, and the master knows.'

FYODOR. Yes, it's about the purchase of some land. That's right.
He's got a visitor with him at the moment. So here's what you
do: you tell them to wait.

DOORKEEPER. Wait? Wait where?

FYODOR. Wait in the yard, and then I'll send for them.

> *The* DOORKEEPER *opens the front door. Enter* TANYA
> *from the pantry, followed by three* PEASANTS *and*
> GRIGORY.

TANYA. Right turn. In here, in here!

FYODOR. I didn't say to let them in here.

GRIGORY. Told you, didn't I? Miss Fidget.

TANYA (*to* FYODOR). Oh, come on, now, they'll be all right.
  They're from home.

FYODOR. They'll walk mud all over the floor.

TANYA. They've wiped their feet. And I'll clear up after them.
  (*To the* PEASANTS.) Look, you stand here.

> *The* PEASANTS *come right into the room. They are
> carrying presents wrapped in handkerchiefs: Easter cakes,
> eggs, and towels. They look round, searching for something.*

GRIGORY. Look at them! They won't be happy till they've
  crossed themselves.

TANYA. This is just an antechamber. There's no icon in here,
  my dears.

GRIGORY. But that picture on the stairs is awful holy.

> *The* PEASANTS *turn towards the staircase and cross
> themselves.*
> *Exit the* DOORKEEPER *through the front door.*
> *The* PEASANTS *bow towards* FYODOR *and stand solidly.*

(*to* FYODOR:) They say that Pironet's is the smart shop for
  boots. But I bet they haven't got a pair as natty as that.
  (*Indicates the* THIRD PEASANT's *boots, which are made out
  of a kind of hemp matting.*)

FYODOR. All you ever do is smirk behind people's backs.

> *Exit* GRIGORY *into the pantry.*

FYODOR (*rises, and crosses to the* PEASANTS). So you're the
  ones from Kursk, about the purchase of the land?

1ST PEASANT. We are so. The matter in hand, broadly speaking,
  touches upon implicating the sale of the land. How might we
  tell him we are here?

FYODOR. I know all about it. You wait here — I'll go and tell
  him.

> *Exit* FYODOR *into the* MASTER's *room.*
> *The* PEASANTS *look round, not knowing where to put
> their presents.*

1ST PEASANT. What's the what-you-may-call-it, the — I don't know — the how-do-you-do you put things on to give them to people? When you do it in proper form, and make a nice proper thing out of it? A saucer, is it?

TANYA. In a moment. Give them here. They can go on this for now. (*Puts them on a little sofa.*)

1ST PEASANT. What station in life would he be, the worthy gentleman who addressed himself to us just now? Broadly speaking?

TANYA. That was Fyodor. He's the valet.

1ST PEASANT. The valet. Of course. In other words, another one of the domestic disposition. (*To* TANYA:) And what about you? Would you also be broadly speaking in service here?

TANYA. One of the maids, me. But, you know, I'm from the Kursk estate as well. And what's more, I know you, and I know *you*. Old Grandad here's the only one I don't know. (*Indicates the* THIRD PEASANT.)

3RD PEASANT. Recognised them, and never recognised me?

TANYA (*to* FIRST PEASANT). You're Yefim Antonich?

1ST PEASANT. Indeed I am.

TANYA (*to* SECOND PEASANT). And you're Zakhar Trifonich? You're Semyon's father?

2ND PEASANT. Right.

3RD PEASANT. Now supposing I tell you I'm Mitry Chilikin. Recognise me now?

TANYA. Now I know you as well.

2ND PEASANT. Whose lass would you be?

TANYA. I'm an orphan. My mother was Aksinya, who married the soldier.

1ST & 3RD PEASANTS (*in surprise*). Well, well, well!

2ND PEASANT. It's right what they say: Give tuppence for a little pig, put little pig in rye; your little pig is pig full big, in two winks of an eye.

1ST PEASANT. True it is. She's a proper little mademoiselle.

3RD PEASANT. So she is, now. Oh lordy me!

VASILY (*rings, off, then calls*). Grigory! Grigory!

1ST PEASANT. Who's that working himself up so?

TANYA. That's the young master.

3RD PEASANT. Oh lord! I told you it would be better to wait outside.

Silence.

2ND PEASANT. You're the one Semyon's marrying?

TANYA. Has he really written to you about it? (*Hides her face in her apron.*)

2ND PEASANT. He's written, all right. I don't know what he's been dreaming up. The lad's been getting himself spoiled, I can see.

TANYA (*warmly*). He's not been getting himself spoiled at all! Shall I send him in to you?

2ND PEASANT. What do you want to be sending him in for? Let me get my breath back. We've got plenty of time!

VASILY (*cries despairingly, off*). Grigory! Where are you, damn you?

Enter VASILY, *in his shirt, and putting on his pince-nez.*

Has everyone dropped dead?

TANYA. He's not here, Mr. Vasily. I'll send him directly. (*Goes towards the pantry door.*)

VASILY. I can hear everyone chattering away out here. What are these scarecrows? Where have they sprung from?

TANYA. They're peasants from the Kursk estate, Mr. Vasily.

VASILY. And who's this? Oh yes, from Bourdet's.

The PEASANTS *bow.* VASILY *pays no attention to them.* TANYA, *going out, meets* GRIGORY *coming in, and remains.*

There you are. I keep telling you — the other boots. I can't wear these!

GRIGORY. But the other ones are standing there too.

VASILY. Where there?

GRIGORY. Right there there.

VASILY. You're lying.

GRIGORY. You'll see.

Exeunt VASILY *and* GRIGORY.

3RD PEASANT. Maybe it's not what you might call the time for
it now. Maybe we should away to find lodgings, and wait a
while.

TANYA. No, you just wait here. It'll be all right. I'll fetch you
some plates to put your presents on.

> *Exit* TANYA.
> *Enter* SAKHATOV *and the* MASTER, *with* FYODOR
> *behind them.*
> *The* PEASANTS *take their presents and strike suitable*
> *attitudes.*

MASTER (*to the* PEASANTS). I'm coming, I'm coming. Just
wait a minute. (*Indicating* BOURDET'S MAN:) Who's this?

BOURDET'S MAN. From Bourdet's.

MASTER. Oh yes. Bourdet's.

SAKHATOV (*smiling*). No, I am not denying it. But you must
agree that in spite of everything you say it is difficult for us
uninitiated brethren to believe.

MASTER. You say: I cannot believe. But we do not even demand
belief. We demand investigation. Look, I cannot *not* believe
in this ring. And this ring I obtained from over there.

SAKHATOV. Over there? Over where?

MASTER. From the other world. Yes!

SAKHATOV (*smiling*). Very interesting. Very interesting.

MASTER. But you, we must assume, think that I'm the sort of
man who is very easily convinced, the sort of man who
imagines things that don't exist. But then there's the Professor
— not, I should say, just anyone, but after all a professor —
and he accepts it. And he's not the only one. How about
Crookes, the pioneer of cathode rays? How about Wallace,
Darwin's fellow-evolutionist?

SAKHATOV. I am not denying it. I am merely saying that is is
very interesting. And it would be very interesting to know how
the Professor explains it.

MASTER. He has his theory, he has his theory! Come along this
evening — he's bound to be there. First we'll have Grossmann.
Do you know Grossmann? The famous clairvoyant?

SAKHATOV. I've heard of him. I've never chanced to see him.

MASTER. Well, then, come along. First Grossmann, then Kapchich the medium, and our seance. (*To* FYODOR:) Has the messenger returned from Kapchich?

FYODOR. Not yet.

MASTER (*to* SAKHATOV). But you come along anyway. If Kapchich isn't there we shall find our own medium. Our good friend Marya Ignatyevna is a medium. Not such a powerful one as Kapchich, but all the same . . .

Enter TANYA, *with the plates for the presents. She listens to the conversation.*

SAKHATOV (*smiling*). Yes, yes. Only there is one rather odd circumstance. Why are the mediums always from the so-called educated classes? Kapchich and Marya Ignatyevna both are. If this were some special power, then one ought to come across it everywhere — among the people, among the peasants.

MASTER. And so you do. One of our peasants, a chap we have about the house here, has turned out to be a medium. We summoned him the other day during a seance — we needed to move a divan — and then we completely forgot about him. He'd probably fallen asleep. Anyway, just imagine, our seance was over — Kapchich had woken up — when suddenly we notice that around this peasant in the other corner of the room psychic phenomena are beginning to occur. The table moved and walked.

TANYA suppresses a laugh.

MASTER. I beg your pardon . . . ? I thought you made some remark.

TANYA shakes her head.

Anyway, this fellow too is evidently a medium. Added to which, in facial appearance he is very like Hume. You remember Hume, the Scottish medium? — a fair-haired, rather simple-minded fellow.

SAKHATOV (*shrugs*). Well, well, well. Most interesting. You should put him to some tests.

MASTER. We are indeed putting him to some tests. And not only

him. There are any number of mediums. It's simply that we
don't know them. Just the other day, for instance, one old
woman — a sick old woman! — moved a stone wall.

SAKHATOV. Moved a stone wall?

MASTER. Yes, yes. She lay there in bed, completely ignorant of
the fact that she was a medium. Put her hand against the wall
— and the wall moved back.

SAKHATOV. And didn't fall down?

MASTER. And didn't fall down.

SAKHATOV. Strange. So I will come along this evening, then.

MASTER. Yes, come along, come along. There will be a seance
whatever happens.

> SAKHATOV *puts his overcoat on.*
> *The* MASTER *accompanies him to the door and sees him
> out.*

BOURDET'S MAN (*to* TANYA) Tell the mistress I'm here,
there's a love. You don't want me to spend the night here, do
you?

TANYA. Wait. She and the young mistress are going for a drive,
so they'll soon be out.

> *Exit* TANYA.
> *The* MASTER *goes up to the* PEASANTS, *who bow and
> offer him their gifts.*

MASTER. We don't need all this business.

1ST PEASANT (*smiling*). But this is our first duty. As according
to what the commune of our village instructed us.

2ND PEASANT. This is how it's done.

3RD PEASANT. Don't think about it, even. We do it because
we're so greatly contented with our, well, let me put it this
way: just as our parents, so to speak, served your parents, so
to speak, so do we wish with all our soul, and not as one
might say in order to kind of so to speak . . . (*Bows.*)

MASTER. Well, what is it? What exactly do you want?

1ST PEASANT. The thing is this, your honour. We want to see
your honour.

PETRISHCHEV *runs in, wearing a greatcoat.*

PETRISHCHEV. Is Vasily awake? (*Sees the* MASTER, *and gives him a brief nod.*)
MASTER. You want my son?
PETRISHCHEV. Yes — Vovo. I just want to see him for a minute.
MASTER. Through here.

PETRISHCHEV *takes off his greatcoat and goes hurriedly into* VASILY's *room.*

(*to the* PEASANTS:) All right. So what is it you want?
2ND PEASANT. Take the presents.
1ST PEASANT (*smiling*). Offered at the behalf of the village.
3RD PEASANT. And don't think about it! What's there to think about? We feel to you as to a father by flesh and blood. Just don't think about it!
MASTER. Well, what difference does it make . . . ? Take them, Fyodor.
FYODOR. Give them here, then. (*Takes the presents.*)
MASTER, So, what is it?
1ST PEASANT. So we want to see your honour.
MASTER. As far as I can see you *are* seeing me. Now, what do you want to see me about?
1ST PEASANT. What we want is to take steps towards implicating the sale of the land. Broadly speaking . . .
MASTER. So what, then — you *are* buying the land, are you?
1ST PEASANT. Indeed. That is indeed what it comes down to. Generally speaking, to be more precise, it's a question of the purchase of the ownership of the land. We are authorised by the commune, speaking by and large, to as how one should say enter into it, in the proper manner, through the good offices of the state bank, and with the affixment thereunto of a revenue stamp in the statutory amount.
MASTER. So you want to buy the land with the help of the bank. Is that it?
1ST PEASANT. That's what it comes down to, just as you yourself proposed to us in the summer. The whole sum, in full, for the purchase of the land comes to, speaking in round figures, thirty-two thousand eight hundred and sixty-four roubles.

MASTER. That's right. But what about payment?

1ST PEASANT. The payment that the commune proposes is as was agreed upon in the summer — by instalments. That's to say with the payment now in ready money, in full accordance with the laws of the land, of four thousand roubles.

2ND PEASANT. In other words, four thousand in cash now, and wait for the rest.

3RD PEASANT (*unfolding the money*). And with this be ever hopeful that we shall pledge ourselves, and that we shall never so to speak in any way as one might say do aught but what we ought.

MASTER. But, look, I wrote to you and said I was agreeable only in the event that you raised all the money.

1ST PEASANT. Indeed, indeed, that would be more acceptable. But it's not within our powers.

MASTER. So what's to be done?

1ST PEASANT. By and large the commune was relying on the fact that as in the summer you made a proposal for repayment by instalments . . .

MASTER. That was last year. Then I agreed, but now I'm unable to.

2ND PEASANT. But how can that be? You raised our hopes, and then we got hold of this paper and collected the money together.

3RD PEASANT. Have mercy on us, father! Our plots are small. Nowhere to turn out a cow, not even a hen. Don't sin against us, father! (*Bows.*)

MASTER. It's true, certainly, that last year I agreed to payment by instalments. But circumstances since then have changed, so that now I find it inconvenient.

2ND PEASANT. Without that land we may as well cut our throats.

1ST PEASANT. Without the land our hold on life will in truth weaken and fall away.

3RD PEASANT (*bows*). Father! Our plots are small. Nowhere to turn out a cow, nor even a cockerel. Father, have mercy on us! Take the money!

MASTER (*looking through the paper they have brought*). I

understand your feelings, and as far as I am personally
concerned I should like to help you. Wait. I shall give you my
answer in half-an-hour. Fyodor, I'm not at home to anyone.

Exit the MASTER.
The PEASANTS *are despondent.*

2ND PEASANT. How do you like that, then? The lot, he says,
give me the lot. But where would we get it from?
1ST PEASANT. If only he hadn't raised our hopes in the summer.
We did indeed count on it being as was in the summer agreed.
3RD PEASANT. Oh lordy me! I'd like already undone the money.
(*Folds it away.*) Now what are we going to do?
FYODOR. How much money have you got?
1ST PEASANT. All told and totted up, four thousand roubles.
FYODOR. There you are, then. Roll up your sleeves and collect
some more.
1ST PEASANT. That's how we collected what we've got, with
our sleeves rolled up. Your notions won't get us very far,
mister.
2ND PEASANT. If the money's not there, you couldn't drag it
out with your teeth.
3RD PEASANT. We got this together with all our heart and soul
and as you might say with a fine toothcomb.

Enter VASILY *and* PETRISHCHEV. *They are both
smoking* papirosy.

VASILY. But I've already said I'll try. I'll try absolutely as hard
as I can, what? ·
PETRISHCHEV. As long as you realise that if you don't get hold
of it there's going to be Lord only knows what kind of a stink.
VASILY. I've said I'll try. And try I jolly well will.
PETRISHCHEV. All right. I'm just telling you — you absolutely
must get your hands on it. I'll wait.

Exit PETRISHCHEV *into* VASILY's *room.*

VASILY (*flaps his hand*). What the deuce am I to do?

The PEASANTS *bow.*

VASILY *gazes at* BOURDET'S MAN.

(*to* FYODOR). Why don't you let this Bourdet's fellow go? He seems to have moved in with us for good, what? Look, he's gone to sleep.

FYODOR. Well, he handed in a note, and they told him to wait. The mistress'll be down some time.

VASILY (*looks at the* PEASANTS, *and sights the money*). What's this? Money? Who's this for? Is this money for us? (*To* FYODOR:) Who are these chaps?

FYODOR. Peasants from Kursk. They're buying some land.

VASILY. Oh. Have we sold it?

FYODOR. No, we haven't agreed on it yet. This lot are being a bit careful with their money.

VASILY. Really? Well, we'll have to persuade them. (*To the* PEASANTS.) So you're buying, what?

1ST PEASANT. Indeed we are proposing to acquire possession of the land's ownership.

VASILY. Well, don't be so tight-fisted about it. Land — it's vital to a peasant, you take it from me. Absolutely vital.

1ST PEASANT. Indeed to a peasant land is the first necessity. That's a fact.

VASILY. So fork out. Because what is land? I'll tell you — land is something you can sow wheat in. You can get nearly two tons an acre. Sixty roubles a ton. Over a hundred roubles an acre. How about that? Or mint. I'll tell you — with mint you can rake in three hundred roubles an acre!

1ST PEASANT. Indeed you can raise all these crops. Anyone with a notion how to do it.

VASILY. So definitely mint. I studied all this, you know. There are books about it. I'll show you.

1ST PEASANT. Indeed, indeed, so far as you're concerned you can see it clearer in books. That's because you've got the brains.

VASILY. So just you cough up the cash and buy away. (*To* FYODOR:) Where's Papa?

FYODOR. He's in. Said not to disturb him.

VASILY. I suppose he's consulting the spirits about whether he should sell the land or not.

FYODOR. I couldn't say. I know he wasn't decided.

VASILY. What do you think, Fyodor — is he in funds at the moment?

FYODOR. Don't know. Hardly likely. What do you want to know for? You took a sizeable slice off him last week.

VASILY. But I laid that out on those dogs. The thing is now, you see, our new club. Because old Petrishchev in there — he's been elected. And I borrowed some money off him, so now I have to kick in for both of us.

FYODOR. What new club's this? Is this the bicycling one?

VASILY. No, listen, I'll tell you — this is a new one. Tremendously serious. It's for encouraging an ancient Russian breed of dog — the borzoi. And do you know who the president of it is?

Exit VASILY *into the* MASTER's *study.*

1ST PEASANT (*to* FYODOR). Who'd that be, then, mister?

FYODOR (*smiling*). The young governor.

3RD PEASANT. The heir, as you might say. Oh lordy me! (*Hides the money.*) I can see I'll have to put this away for a bit.

1ST PEASANT. From what we heard he was a military man. In the cavalry, or some such.

FYODOR. No, he's an only son, so he's excused military service.

3RD PEASANT. Left, as they say, to support his parents.

2ND PEASANT (*shakes his head*). Him support his parents? That's a good one.

3RD PEASANT. Oh my lord!

Enter VASILY, *with the* MASTER *in the doorway behind him.*

VASILY. It's always the same! Really, it's amazing. First they say to me why haven't I got anything to keep me occupied, and then as soon as I've found something to do and I am occupied, and we've founded a club, a serious club with high-minded aims — then they begrudge me a measly three hundred roubles!

MASTER. I've told you I can't, and I can't. I haven't got it.

VASILY. But, look, you've sold that land.

MASTER. In the first place, I haven't sold it, and in the second place and above all — leave me in peace. You've been told, haven't you? I'm busy. (*Slams the door.*)

FYODOR. I told you it wasn't the moment.

VASILY. Well, I must say, this is a fine state of affairs. I'll go and see Mama. That's my only salvation. This one's going dotty over his spiritualism. He's forgotten about all the rest of us.

> VASILY *goes upstairs.*

> FYODOR *is about to sit down with the newspaper when* BETSY, *the daughter of the house, and* MARYA, *the music teacher, come downstairs, followed by* GRIGORY.

BETSY. Is the carriage ready?

GRIGORY. It's being got out.

BETSY (*to* MARYA). Come on! It's him!

MARYA. Him?

BETSY. I saw him!

MARYA. Saw whom?

BETSY. You know perfectly well — Petrishchev.

MARYA. Then where is he?

BETSY. In Vovo's room. You'll see.

MARYA. But supposing it's not him?

> *The* PEASANTS *and the* BOURDET'S MAN *bow.*

BETSY. Oh, you're from Bourdet's, with the dress?

BOURDET'S MAN. That's right. Will you give orders I can go?

BETSY. Oh, I know nothing about it. That's up to Mama.

BOURDET'S MAN. I don't know who it's up to. I was told to take it round and get the money.

BETSY. Well, then, just wait.

MARYA. Is it that costume for the charade?

BETSY. Yes, that absolutely darling costume. But Mama won't accept it. She refuses to pay for it.

MARYA. But why ever not?

BETSY. Ask her! Paying 500 roubles for Vovo, for those dogs of his — that's nothing. But a hundred roubles for a dress — that's apparently a fortune. But I can't go on and perform looking like a scarecrow! (*Sees the* PEASANTS.) Who on earth are these creatures?

GRIGORY. Peasants, buying some land or other.

BETSY. Oh, I thought they were hunters. Some hunters were supposed to be coming to see Vovo. Aren't you hunters?

1ST PEASANT. Not at all, miss, not by any manner of means. We are here to see the master, on account of the completion of the sale of the deed or title to a certain piece of land.

BETSY. Are you sure you're not hunters?

The PEASANTS *remain silent.*

Oh, what idiots! (*Goes to the door of* VASILY's *room.*) Vovo! (*Laughs.*)

MARYA. But we just met him going upstairs.

BETSY. Yes, but you don't have to *remember* that, do you? Vovo, are you there?

Enter PETRISHCHEV, *from* VASILY's *room.*

PETRISHCHEV. Vovo's not here, but I am, and I'm more than ready to serve you in his place. Good day to you. And good day to you, Miss Marya. (*Takes first* BETSY's *hand, then* MARYA's, *and shakes them long and hard.*)

2ND PEASANT. Look at him. You'd think he was pumping water.

BETSY. You're no substitute, but still you're better than nothing. (*Laughs.*) What's this business you've got with Vovo?

PETRISHCHEV. Oh, financial business. Something to do with a Finn.

BETSY. A Finn?

PETRISHCHEV. A Finn, yes. And an Ancial. It's Finn-Ancial business.

BETSY. What's an Ancial?

PETRISHCHEV. Oh, honestly! That's the whole point, that it doesn't mean anything!

BETSY. Well, I think that's *feeble!* (*Laughs.*)

PETRISHCHEV. You can't make them work out every time, you know. It's a sort of lottery. You keep going in for them, and then suddenly you come up with a winner.

Exit FYODOR *into the* MASTER's *study.*

BETSY. Well, that one was just feeble. But listen, did you go to the Mergasovs' last night?

PETRISHCHEV. I did, but not so much to *mère* Gasov as to *père* Gasov. And somewhat less to père Gasov than to Gasov *fils*.

BETSY. Can't you say *anything* without turning it into a pun? It's a positive disease! But did they have the Gypsy singers there?

PETRISHCHEV (*sings*). 'And on her skirts blazed cockerels with golden combs . . . '

BETSY. Oh, you are lucky! We were so bored at Fofo's!

PETRISHCHEV. 'And she swore a Gypsy oath that when the moon was high, she would . . . ' How does it go? Miss Marya, what's the next bit?

MARYA. 'Stay one hour with me.'

PETRISHCHEV. I *beg* your pardon, Miss Marya? (*Laughs.*)

BETSY. *Cessez, vous devenez impossible!*

PETRISHCHEV. *J'ai cessé. J'ai cessé, j'ai dédé, j'ai féfé . . . j'ai bébé!*

BETSY. I know one way of sparing us your witticisms, and that's to make you sing. Let's go into Vovo's room — he's got a guitar in there. Come on, Marya!

> *Exeunt* BETSY, MARYA *and* PETRISHCHEV *into* VASILY's *room.*

1ST PEASANT. Whose lasses are they?

GRIGORY. One's the young mistress. The other one's the mademoiselle who teaches her music.

1ST PEASANT. Implicates her education, as you might say. Very neat, isn't she? Very neat and tidy. Proper oil painting.

2ND PEASANT. Why don't they marry her off? She's of marrying years, surely to God?

GRIGORY. What, like with you people? Fifteen, and you're straight into it.

1ST PEASANT. What about the little funny fellow, then? Is he one of those musician sort of people, too?

GRIGORY (*mimics him*). 'One of those musician sort of people'! You don't understand anything!

1ST PEASANT. Indeed, that's our foolishness, that's our uneducatedness.

3RD PEASANT. Oh lordy lordy me.

> *The sound of Gypsy songs to the guitar comes from*
> VASILY's *room.*

> *Enter* SEMYON, *with* TANYA *following him. She watches*
> *over the meeting of father and son.*

GRIGORY (*to* SEMYON). What do you want?

SEMYON. They sent me round to Mr. Kapchich.

GRIGORY. Well, what's the answer?

SEMYON. He said to say, this evening he can't manage it.

GRIGORY. Right, I'll tell him.

> *Exit* GRIGORY *into the* MASTER's *study.*

SEMYON. Hello, father. Hello, Uncle Yefim, Uncle Mitty.
   Everyone all right at home?

2ND PEASANT. They're all right.

1ST PEASANT. Hello, Semyon.

3RD PEASANT. Still in the land of the living, then?

SEMYON (*smiling*). Well, then, father, what do you think? Shall
   we go and take a dish of tea?

2ND PEASANT. Hold on till we're through with our business.
   Can't you see we're busy now?

SEMYON. Right, then, I'll be waiting on the back porch.

TANYA (*runs after him*). Why didn't you say anything?

SEMYON. How can I say it now, in front of everyone? Don't
   rush me. We'll go and drink tea. Then I'll say.

> *Exit* SEMYON *into pantry.*

> *Enter* FYODOR *and* GRIGORY. FYODOR *sits down at*
> *the window with his newspaper.*

1ST PEASANT. Well, then, mister, how's our business coming
   along?

FYODOR. Hold on — he'll be out directly. He's just finishing.

TANYA. How do you know?

FYODOR. I know when he's coming to the end of the questions,
   because he reads through all the questions and answers aloud.

TANYA. Is it really true you can talk to the spirits with a saucer?

FYODOR. Apparently.

TANYA. So what, if they tell him to sign, he goes ahead and signs?

FYODOR. How else?

TANYA. But they don't talk to him in words, do they?

FYODOR. In letters. Whatever letter of the alphabet it stops against, he notes it down.

TANYA. Yes, but supposing it's at one of these seances . . . ?

Enter the MASTER.

MASTER. Well, my friends, I cannot do it. Much as I should like to, I simply cannot. If you had all the money, it would be another matter.

1ST PEASANT. Indeed it would be better. But the people are poor, and it's not possible, not by any manner of means.

MASTER. I cannot do it. I simply cannot. Here's your paper. I cannot sign it.

3RD PEASANT. Have pity on us, father! Have mercy on us!

2ND PEASANT. Behaving like that! It's an insult.

MASTER. My dear good chaps, there's no insult about it. I told you back in the summer: if you want to do it, do it. You *didn't* want to then, and now it's impossible for me.

3RD PEASANT. Father! Have Mercy! How are we to live now? Our plots are small. Nowhere to turn out a cow, not even a hen.

The MASTER *turns to go, but remains standing in the doorway of his study.*

Enter, down the stairs, the MISTRESS, *tight-laced and wearing a hat. With her is the* DOCTOR, *and behind them comes* VASILY, *in a cheerful and playful frame of mind, putting money away in his wallet.*

MISTRESS. So I'm to go on taking it?

DOCTOR. If you have a recurrence of the symptoms, then go on taking it by all means. But the main thing is, you must behave. How can you expect a thick syrup to pass through a fine hair-like tube when you're squeezing the tube even tighter? It

can't be done! Well, that's how it is with the bile duct. It's
all very simple, you know.

MISTRESS. Yes, yes, yes. All right.

DOCTOR. 'All right,' you say, and on you go exactly as before.
But it can't be done, Ma'am, it can't be done. Well, then, I
shall bid you good-day.

MISTRESS. Only until this evening. I shall expect you then all
the same. Without you I shall never have the resolution.

DOCTOR. Very well, very well. If time permits I shall be back.

Exit the DOCTOR.

MISTRESS (*sees the* PEASANTS). What's this? What is all this?
What are these people supposed to be?

The PEASANTS *bow.*

FYODOR. They're peasants from the Kursk estate. They've come
to see the master about the purchase of some land.

MISTRESS. I can see they're peasants, but who on earth let them
in?

FYODOR. The master said to. He's just been talking to them
about the sale of the land.

MISTRESS. What sale of what land? There's no earthly need to
go selling anything. But what chiefly concerns me is how
anyone could let people into the house off the street. How
could they do it? Straight off the street like that! People who've
spent the night God knows where! Every fold of their clothes
laden with germs! Scarlet fever germs, smallpox germs,
diphtheria germs! And great heavens — they're from *Kursk!*
There's a diphtheria epidemic in Kursk! Doctor! Doctor! Fetch
the doctor back!

Exit the MASTER *into his study, closing the door.*

Exit GRIGORY *and* TANYA *in search of the* DOCTOR.

VASILY. Don't worry, Mama. Would you like me to fumigate
them? (*Blows smoke over the* PEASANTS.) That'll give all
those germs something to think about, what?

The MISTRESS *maintains a stern silence.*

(*to the* PEASANTS). Have you tried raising pigs, by the way? There's an awful lot of money in pigs.

1ST PEASANT. Indeed, we go in for the pig-raising side of things whenever we can.

VASILY. This sort of chappie . . . (*Grunts like a piglet.*)

MISTRESS. Vovo! Vovo! Stop that!

VASILY. Have I got it? What? What?

1ST PEASANT. Certainly. To the life.

MISTRESS. Vovo, I'm warning you! Stop it at once!

2ND PEASANT. What's the use?

3RD PEASANT. I said we should have gone and found lodgings for the time being.

Enter DOCTOR *and* GRIGORY.

DOCTOR. Now what is it?

MISTRESS. Here you are telling me to avoid excitement, but how can I stay calm? I take the utmost precautions with any visitor there might be doubts about — my own sister I haven't seen for two months — then, what do you think? All of a sudden there are people from Kursk — straight from Kursk, where there's a diphtheria epidemic raging — and there they are in the middle of my house!

DOCTOR. You mean these stout fellows?

MISTRESS. Yes — straight from the infected area!

DOCTOR. If they're from a district where there's an ouybreak of diphtheria then of course it was imprudent to invite them in. But all the same there's no call to get so very excited.

MISTRESS. What, when you yourself are always prescribing caution?

DOCTOR. Yes, yes, yes — but there's no need to get quite as excited as this.

MISTRESS. What, when I'm going to have to have the whole house disinfected from top to bottom?

DOCTOR. Why do you want the whole house disinfected? It costs far too much — 300 roubles, and it might run to more than that. I'm going to suggest something very cheap but entirely practical. Just take a large bottle of water . . .

MISTRESS. Boiled water?

DOCTOR. No matter. Very well, then, boiled water. Then add
to the water a table-spoonful of salicylic acid. Have everything
washed that they've so much as touched. And of course get
these fine fellows themselves out of here. That's all. Then —
don't worry. You might spray two or three glassfuls of the
same mixture into the air with an atomizer. You'll see how
agreeable it will be. And completely safe!
MISTRESS. Where's Tanya? Call Tanya!

Enter TANYA.

TANYA. Ma'am?
MISTRESS. You know the big bottle in the lavatory?
TANYA. The one you disinfected the laundrywoman with
yesterday?
MISTRESS. Of course — which one do you think I mean? First
wash where they're standing with soap, then with the mixture
in the bottle.
TANYA. Very good, Ma'am. I know the way.
MISTRESS. Then take the atomizer . . . No, I'll come back and
do it myself.
DOCTOR. That's the style. And have no fear. Well, then, until
this evening.

Exit DOCTOR.

MISTRESS. Them — out, out! Get the smell of them away from
here. Out! Out! Out! What are you staring at?
1ST PEASANT. The thing was this. We in our like foolishness,
being like invited to come in . . .
GRIGORY (*ushering the* PEASANTS *out fo the front door*). All
right, then — off you go.
2ND PEASANT. What about my handkerchief? It's round the
cakes I gave him.
3RD PEASANT. Oh lordy me. I said lodgings was the place to go.

GRIGORY *throws him out after the others.*

BOURDET'S MAN. So what's the answer going to be?
MISTRESS. Ah, you're the one from Bourdet's? (*Becomes
excited.*) The answer is that there's no answer! And take the

thing back! I told her I hadn't ordered the costume! I told her I wouldn't allow any daughter of mine to wear such a thing!

BOURDET'S MAN. Look, I don't know anything about it. They just sent me round.

MISTRESS. Off you go! Off, off, off! And take it back! I shall call in myself.

VASILY (*ceremoniously*). Your Excellency the Ambassador of Bourdet — trot along.

BOURDET'S MAN. You could have told me all this a long time ago. Why have I been sitting here for five hours?

VASILY. Your Bourdet-an Excellency — scoot.

MISTRESS. Stop that, Vovo, please.

Exit the BOURDET'S MAN.

Betsy! Where is that daughter of mine? I'm perpetually waiting for her.

VASILY (*shouts at the top of his voice*). Betsy! Petrishchev! Come here! And sharp about it, what?

Enter BETSY, MARYA *and* PETRISHCHEV.

MISTRESS. Where have you been? I'm perpetually waiting for you.

BETSY. On the contrary — I'm waiting for you.

PETRISHCHEV *gives the* MISTRESS *a mere nod, and kisses her hand.*

MISTRESS. Good day. (*To* BETSY.) And always answering back!

BETSY. Mama, if you're out of temper it would be better if I didn't come with you.

MISTRESS. Look, are we going or aren't we?

BETSY. If we're going let's go. What are we waiting for?

MISTRESS. Did you see what came from Bourdet's?

BETSY. Yes, I did see, and I was absolutely delighted. I ordered that costume, and as soon as someone has paid for it I'm going to wear it.

MISTRESS. I'm not going to pay for it and I'm not going to

allow you to wear it. It's indecent.

BETSY. Why has it suddenly become indecent? One moment it's perfectly decent, and the next moment you've had an attack of prudishness.

MISTRESS. It's not a question of prudishness. Remake the whole bodice, and then you could wear it.

BETSY. Mama, that's utterly impossible.

MISTRESS. Well, then, put your things on.

They sit down. GRIGORY *puts their boots on.*

VASILY. Miss Marya! Do you see how full of emptiness this room is?

MARYA. What about it? (*Starts to laugh already.*)

VASILY. It's been disemBourdet-ed. Good one, what?

MISTRESS. Well, we're off. Tanya!

TANYA. Ma'am?

MISTRESS. Make sure that Fifka doesn't catch cold while I'm out. She's not entirely well. So if she asks to be let out, be sure to put her little yellow overcoat on.

TANYA. Very good, Ma'am.

Exeunt the MISTRESS, BETSY, MARYA, *and* GRIGORY.

PETRISHCHEV. So — did you get it?

VASILY. Only with the utmost labour, I can tell you. First I whizzed in to see the old man. He just snarled and slung me out. So then I went round to the old lady — and, well, I got it. Right here! (*Slaps his pocket.*) Once I've got my teeth into something I don't let go. The grip of the dead, what? You know they're bringing my wolfhounds today?

PETRISHCHEV *and* VASILY *put their coats on. Exeunt.*

Exit TANYA *after them.*

FYODOR (*alone*). Troubles, nothing but troubles. How is it they can't live in harmony? The younger generation — they're not the same. That's the truth of the matter. And women ruling the roost. Like just then the master would have intervened, only he saw she was in her ecstasies, so he closed the door on

her. A man of rare goodness. Rare goodness . . . What's this?
That Tanya's bringing them back again!

Enter TANYA *and the three* PEASANTS.

TANYA. Come in, come in. You'll be all right.

FYODOR. What have you brought them back for?

TANYA. Oh, come on, now. We've got to do something for them
one way or another. And I'm going to be washing the floor
afterwards anyway.

FYODOR. The deal isn't going to be done, I can tell you that.

1ST PEASANT. How can we implicate the business, then, mister?
If your honour would like to put yourself out for us, why, we,
on behalf of the commune, would be ready to show our
gratitude in very substantial manner.

FYODOR. I'm sorry for you, lads, but I don't know. I understand
you right enough. But he's refused, you see. So now what?
The mistress is against it, too. It's long odds, all right. Well,
give me the paper, then. I'll go and have a try. I'll go and ask
him.

Exit FYODOR *into the* MASTER's. *The* PEASANTS *sigh.*

TANYA. All you want is that the master should sign the paper,
yes?

1ST PEASANT. Nothing but that he should put his hand to it,
and sign, and take the money, and there's the lid on it.

TANYA. Wait and see what Fyodor says. If he hasn't persuaded
him, I'll try a little trick.

1ST PEASANT. Circumbobulate him?

TANYA. Try to.

3RD PEASANT. That's the girl. Going to put her shoulder to the
wheel for us, she is. Only bring this off for us, and we'll pledge
ourselves to feed you on the village all your life. How about
that?

1ST PEASANT. If you can just implicate our business, why then
indeed we'll weigh you down with gold.

2ND PEASANT. No two ways about it.

TANYA. I'm not making any promises. You know what they say:
'It's never any harm to ask . . .

1ST PEASANT. . . . nor any shame to try the task.' That's certainly true.

Enter FYODOR.

FYODOR. It's no use, lads. He wouldn't agree and he won't agree. Take your paper, and away you go.

1ST PEASANT (*takes the paper. To* TANYA). So now we must more or less rely on you.

TANYA. Leave it to me. You go and wait in the street, and in a minute I'll run out and tell you what.

Exeunt the PEASANTS *through the front door.*

Fyodor, be a dear, and ask the master to step out here. I need to have a word with him.

FYODOR. Why, what's going on?

TANYA. I just need to, that's all. Please ask him. I'm not up to anything wrong, truly.

FYODOR. What is it, then?

TANYA. A little secret. I'll tell you afterwards. Just you ask him.

FYODOR (*smiling*). What you're about I can't imagine. But all right, then, I'll tell him.

Exit FYODOR *into the* MASTER's *study.*

TANYA (*alone*). I'm going to do it. I really am. Well, didn't he say himself that Semyon's got the power? And don't I know how it's done? When the table moved before, no one guessed that was me under there. So now I'll tell Semyon what to do. And if it doesn't work, we'll be no worse off. It can't be such a terrible sin, can it?

Enter the MASTER, *followed by* FYODOR.

MASTER (*smiling*). So here's the petitioner! What is it you want, my dear?

TANYA. It's a little secret, sir. May I speak to you alone?

MASTER. What can it be? Fyodor, will you leave us for a minute?

Exit FYODOR *into the pantry.*

TANYA. Sir, I've lived and grown up in your house, and I'm very grateful to you for everything. So now I'm going to confide in you, just as if you were my own father. It's about Semyon, who also lives in your house. He wants to marry me.

MASTER. Does he, indeed?

TANYA. I'm telling you what's in my heart, just like I would before God. Being an orphan I've no one to advise me.

MASTER. Come, come — what do you need advice for? He seems to be a good enough young chap.

TANYA. That's right, and I'd have no worries over him at all — only there's just one thing I'm a bit doubtful about. And that's what I want to ask you. Because there's one thing thing about him that I can't make out whether it would be something wrong or not.

MASTER. He drinks, does he?

TANYA. No, he doesn't, thanks be to God. But since I know that there's such a thing as spirituality . . .

MASTER. You know that, do you?

TANYA. Of course! I understand all that perfectly well. Some people don't understand, it's true, but that's because they're uneducated.

MASTER. So what about it?

TANYA. I'm frightened on account of Semyon. Because it happens with him.

MASTER. What happens?

TANYA. Why, this sort of like spirituality. You ask the servants. Let him just happen to nod off while he's sitting at table, and at once the table starts to tremble and all kind of creak. Like so: tk, t . . . tk! All the servants have heard it.

MASTER. This is exactly what I was saying to Sakhatov this morning. Go on.

TANYA. Anyway . . . when was it . . . ? Yes, on Wednesday. We were just sitting down to dinner. He'd only just sat down to table when — hup! — the spoon's come to his hand, all by itself!

MASTER. Now this is interesting. Jumped into his hand? What, had he dozed off?

TANYA. That I didn't notice. I think, yes, he had.

MASTER. Go on.

TANYA. Well, I'm frightened, and I wanted to ask if any harm could come of it. How would you like to live your life with such things going on?

MASTER (*smiling*). Have no fear, there's nothing wrong. It merely signifies that he is a *medium*. Simply a medium. In fact I already knew he was.

TANYA. So that's what it is. And I was so frightened!

MASTER. Have no fear. It's perfectly all right. In fact it is excellent news. Our regular medium won't be here for the seance tonight, so instead we'll do some tests with your young man. No, my dear, don't worry — he'll be a good husband, and so on. This is a special power, and it's present in everyone. It's simply weaker in some, and stronger in others.

TANYA. I'm so grateful. Now I won't think about it any more. I was so frightened! That's what comes of all this ignorance of ours!

MASTER. Have no fear, have no fear. Fyodor!

Enter FYODOR *from the pantry.*

I'm going out. Will you make sure everything is ready for the seance this evening?

FYODOR. But you know Kapchich can't be here . . .

MASTER. That won't matter. (*Puts on his overcoat.*) We shall be holding a trial seance with our own medium.

Exit the MASTER *through the front door, accompanied by* FYODOR.

TANYA (*alone*). He swallowed it! He swallowed the lot! (*She squeals and jumps up and down.*) Great heavens above, he swallowed it all! There's a miracle! (*Squeals.*) Now I'll go through with it, if only Semyon doesn't come over all timid.

Enter FYODOR.

FYODOR. Well, then, did you tell him your secret?

TANYA. I did. And I'll tell you, too — only afterwards. But listen, I've got something I want you to do for me as well.

FYODOR. What's that?

TANYA (*shyly*). You've been like a second father to me. I'm
   going to tell you what's in my heart just like I would before
   God.

FYODOR. Don't beat about the bush, then. What is it?

TANYA. What is it? What it is, is that Semyon wants to marry me.

FYODOR. Does he, indeed? That's something I've been keeping
   my eye open for.

TANYA. Why should I go hiding it? I'm an orphan, that's my
   situation, and you know well enough the way people behave
   in the city here. They keep pestering you, if only it's Grigory
   never giving me a moment's peace. But then, it's this one as
   well . . . (*Indicates* VASILY's *room.*) You know who I mean?
   They seem to think I haven't a soul of my own — that I've
   just been put here for their amusement.

FYODOR. You're no fool, I'll say that for you. So what is it you
   want?

TANYA. Well, Semyon wrote to his father, and no sooner does
   his father set eyes on me today than he says, 'He's spoilt!
   The boy's spoilt!' Take my father's place and talk to the old
   man. Talk to Semyon's father. I could take them into the
   kitchen. Then you could just look in and have a word with
   him.

FYODOR (*smiling*). It's a marriage-broker I'm to be now, is it?
   Well, it might be managed.

TANYA. Fyodor, my dear, take the place of my real father, and
   I'll pray to God for you all the days of my life.

FYODOR. All right, all right. I'll have a word with him by and by.
   I promise. (*Picks up the newspaper.*)

TANYA. You'll be a second father to me.

FYODOR. Yes, yes, yes.

TANYA. So I'll live in hope.

   Exit TANYA *into the pantry.*

FYODOR (*alone*). She's a sweet-natured girl, a good girl. And
   when you think how many just such as her come to their
   downfall. One slip — and then they go from hand to hand like
   worn coins. And afterwards, in all that sea of mud you'd never
   find them. Like that Natasha, who was here before her. She

was a good girl, too, a kind-hearted girl, with a mother who bore her and cherished her and brought her up . . . (*Picks up the paper.*) Well, now, what are they playing at down there in Bulgaria today? How's that good King Ferdinand of theirs worming his way out of it this time . . . ?

Curtain.

Act Two

The servants' kitchen.

The PEASANTS, *coats off and sweating, are sitting at the table drinking tea.* FYODOR *sits smoking a cigar on the other side of the room. Above the stove, out of sight at the beginning of the act, lies the* OLD COOK.

FYODOR. My advice is not to stand in his way. If it's his desire and hers too, then God be with them. She's a good honest girl. She likes to dress smartly, but pay no heed to that. That's the way it is in the city. You can't get by without it. But she's a sensible girl.

2ND PEASANT. Well, if that's what he wants. He's the one who's got to live with her, not me. Only she's almighty clean. How could you take her into a peasant's home? She wouldn't let her mother-in-law so much as look at her.

FYODOR. That, my friend, is not a question of cleanness. That's a question of character. If her character be sound, why then she'll be humble and respectful.

2ND PEASANT. Well, I suppose if the boy's got himself so caught up in her toils then there's nothing for it but to take her. Living with a wife he didn't love would be misery no less. I'll have a word with the old lady, and then God be with them.

FYODOR. Well, then, let's shake on it.

2ND PEASANT. I can see that's the way things are.

1ST PEASANT. Fortune's got her eye on you today, Zakhar. You came but for to do business, and look at you — you've picked yourself out a real beauty for a daughter-in-law. All you want now is to drink on it, just to make it formal like.

FYODOR. That we don't need by any manner of means.

An awkward silence.

I'll tell you something, though. I understand the life you peasants lead. I sometimes turn over in my mind where I could buy a piece of ground myself. Build myself a bit of a house. Live off the land. Maybe in your part of the world.

2ND PEASANT. It's the life.

1ST PEASANT. Indeed, in the country — with money in your pocket — you can have aught the heart might desire.

3RD PEASANT. True enough. The country life's a free one, any day of the year. Not like your town life.

FYODOR. So what — would you accept me as one of yourselves if I came and settled there?

2ND PEASANT. Why shouldn't we accept you? Buy the old men a few drinks — they'll accept you straight off.

1ST PEASANT. But open a tavern, for example, and you'll have such a life you won't want to die. You'll live like a king, and that's all there is to it.

FYODOR. We'll see about that once I get there. All I want to do is to live peacefully in my old age. Not that I don't live well here. Sad to leave it. The master's a man of rare goodness.

1ST PEASANT. Indeed, indeed. But how is it with our business? Is it really come to nothing?

FYODOR. He'd be glad to do it, if it was himself.

2ND PEASANT. You can see he's afraid of his wife.

FYODOR. He's not afraid of her. But then again, there's no harmony there, neither.

3RD PEASANT. If you could just have another try for us, uncle . . . Else how are we to live?

FYODOR. We'll see what comes of Tanya's efforts, though. Since she's set her mind to it.

3RD PEASANT (*drinks tea*). Have mercy on us, uncle! Our plots are small. Nowhere to turn out a cow, not even a hen.

FYODOR. Well, if the matter was in my hands . . . (*To the* 2ND PEASANT.) So, you and I are going to be fathers-in-law together. Have we finished our business about Tanya?

2ND PEASANT. I've already said, so far as I'm concerned, and drink to it or no I won't go back on it. If only we'd settled that other business, though.

Enter the PRESENT COOK.

PRESENT COOK (*to* FYODOR). You know what? Semyon was

in the white kitchen just now and they called him upstairs. The master it was, and that one that raises spirits with him, the bald one. They sat him down and they told him he'd got to perform in place of that Kapchich fellow.

FYODOR. What stories are you telling us now?

PRESENT COOK. What do you mean, stories? Yakov was just telling Tanya.

FYODOR. Well, that's a funny thing for them to do, then.

Enter the COACHMAN.

What do you want?

COACHMAN (*to* FYODOR). You go and tell him. I'm not employed to live with dogs, tell him. Anybody else want to, fine, but me — live with dogs — no.

FYODOR. Dogs? What dogs?

COACHMAN. They've brought three dogs across from the young master and put them with us in the coach-house. They're howling. They've done their dirt everywhere. And you can't get near them or they'll have a piece out of you. They're evil-tempered brutes. Just so much as look at them and they'll eat you. I'd like to take a lump of wood and break their legs.

FYODOR. But when was this?

COACHMAN. Today — they brought them from a dog show. Some expensive breed or other. Boar's-ears, is it? Bear's-eyes? Anyway, to hell with them. Either it's the coachmen living in the coach house, or it's the dogs. So you tell him.

FYODOR. Yes, that's not the way to do things. I'll go and ask about it.

COACHMAN. They could come in here, in the black kitchen, with her.

PRESENT COOK (*angrily*). The servants eat in here, and you want to shut dogs up with them. It's bad enough as it is.

COACHMAN. And I've got the ulsters and the rugs and the harness — they want all that kept clean. Put them in the yardman's lodge. What's wrong with that?

FYODOR. You'll have to tell the young master.

COACHMAN. I'd like to see him walking round with those damned dogs hanging round his neck. Except he doesn't walk anywhere, that one. He fancies himself as a horseman. And what does he do to the horses? He's ruined Dandy, for no reason at all. And he was a good horse! Ekh, what a life!

Exit COACHMAN, *banging the door.*

FYODOR. Yes, it's not the way. It's not the way at all. Well, there we are then, lads. I'll see you later.
PEASANTS. God go with you.

Exit FYODOR.

2ND PEASANT. He looks well-fed, anyway. You'd think he was the grand high admiral.
PRESENT COOK. You're not far wrong, either. His own room, the laundry on him all paid for by the masters, his tea and sugar — all from the masters, his food from their table.
OLD COOK. He's in clover, all right. It's downright robbery.
2ND PEASANT. Who's that on the stove there?
PRESENT COOK. Oh him. He's just someone.

Silence.

1ST PEASANT. All of you here, too, if it comes to that. I was watching you back then, and you supped your way through a tidy few kopecks' worth.
PRESENT COOK. We can't complain. She doesn't stint you on your food. White bread on Sundays, fish on holidays in Lent. And anyone that doesn't want to keep the fast, there's always milk and meat.
2ND PEASANT. You mean there's some that break the fast?
PRESENT COOK. Oh, near enough the lot of them. The only ones that fast are the coachman — not him that came in just then, the old one — and Semyon, and me, and the housekeeper. The rest go on eating anything they like.
2ND PEASANT. And what about himself?
PRESENT COOK. The master? Oh, he tried it once. But he's forgotten what fasting is.
3RD PEASANT. Oh my lord!
1ST PEASANT. All this business of being the gentry — they get it out of books. That's where all their brains come from.

3RD PEASANT. A good barley loaf every day, I'll wager.

PRESENT COOK. A barley loaf? They've never so much as set eyes on nothing but wheaten bread! You should see the food they eat. What haven't they got!

1ST PEASANT. All light and airy, the gentry's food. It's a known fact.

PRESENT COOK. Light and airy or not, they go at it healthy enough.

1ST PEASANT. They're in good appetite, like.

PRESENT COOK. That's why they keep swilling. Sweet wines, vodkas, fizzy liqueurs — there's one to go with every dish. Eat and swill it down. Eat and swill it down.

1ST PEASANT. That's what carries the food through in what you might call the right proportion.

PRESENT COOK. They go at it like nobody's business — it's terrible. With them it's not as if they sat down, ate their food, crossed themselves, and got up again. They eat without stop!

2ND PEASANT. Like pigs — into the trough with their feet.

PRESENT COOK. God bless us, no sooner have they sat up in bed and rubbed their eyes than it's samovar, tea, coffee, chocolate. No sooner have they drunk the first two samovars dry than you're putting the third one down. And now it's lunch, and now it's dinner, and now it's coffee again! And no sooner have they polished that off than straight away it's more tea! And now here come a few little snacks — and sweets, and mint cakes — and there's no end to it! They even lie in bed and eat!

3RD PEASANT. That's the way, now. (*Laughs.*)

2ND PEASANT (*to* FIRST). What's the matter with him?

3RD PEASANT. Just to live one single little day like that!

2ND PEASANT. So when do they do their business, then?

PRESENT COOK. What business? Cards and piano-playing — that's all the business they've got. The young mistress, no sooner has she rubbed her eyes than she's off to the piano, and away she goes! And the other one, the one that lives here, the one that teaches her, she stands and waits till the piano's free. Soon as it comes along, *she* jumps aboard. Sometimes they put two pianos side by side, yes, and with two people on each

of them, so you get four of them hammering away together.
The noise they make, you can hear it from here.

3RD PEASANT. Oh my lord!

PRESENT COOK. That's all the business they've got — piano-
playing and cards. And when people come to the house, why
then it's cards directly — it's wine — it's smoking — and on it
goes the whole night. And as soon as they get up next morning
— they're off on the eating again!

Enter SEMYON.

SEMYON. Sugar in your tea!

1ST PEASANT. Sit down, lad. Come and have a cup.

SEMYON (*goes to the table*). Thanks.

1ST PEASANT *pours him tea.*

2ND PEASANT. Where have you been?

SEMYON. Upstairs.

2ND PEASANT. Why, what's going on up there?

SEMYON. You couldn't make it out. I don't know what to say.

2ND PEASANT. What kind of thing?

SEMYON. I really and truly don't know what to say! They were
testing some kind of power in me. But I couldn't understand
it for the life of me. Tanya says, go ahead. She says, we're
going to try and do something for our peasants, she says,
about that land, to make him sell it.

2ND PEASANT. How's she going to do that?

SEMYON. I can't get it out of her. She's not saying. Just do as I
tell you, she says.

2ND PEASANT. Do what?

SEMYON. Well, nothing so far. They sat me down, they turned
out the light, and they told me to go to sleep. And then Tanya
goes and hides. They can't see her. But I can see her all right.

2ND PEASANT. So what's all this for, then?

SEMYON. Lord knows. You couldn't make out.

1ST PEASANT. It's for passing the time — it's a well-known fact.

2ND PEASANT. Well, I can see you and I are never going to get
to the bottom of this business. Now you tell me something:
how much money have you managed to pick up here?

SEMYON. Twenty-eight roubles, it must be now. But I didn't pick it up — I earned it.

2ND PEASANT. All right, then. Now if God grant we get this business about the land settled, I'll take you home.

SEMYON. Suit me well enough.

2ND PEASANT. You've been spoiled, I'll lay. Won't want to put your hand to the plough, will you?

SEMYON. The plough? Just let me get down to it. Ploughing, mowing — once you've got all that in your hands it doesn't slip out again.

1ST PEASANT. Won't exactly lure you, though, will it, all that, after your city life?

SEMYON. I can live in the country as well, never you fear.

1ST PEASANT. But here's your Uncle Dmitry wants to take your place and try the dainty life.

SEMYON. He'd get sick of it soon enough. It looks easy, but there's a lot of running around in it, too. You get tired out.

PRESENT COOK (*to* 3RD PEASANT.) You should see the dance's and balls they have. You'd get a shock.

3RD PEASANT. What, they'd still be eating?

PRESENT COOK. How could they be eating? You should take a look at what goes on! Fyodor got me into one of them, and I took a real good look. Swarms of ladies, all dressed up to the nines — all done up like nobody's business. Their arms all bare. And all bare here!

3RD PEASANT. Oh my lord!

2ND PEASANT. Pshsh! Lot of filth!

1ST PEASANT. The thing is, the climate's milder here.

PRESENT COOK. So anyway, I looked round and I thought: what is all this? — it's all nakedness! Even the old ones, would you believe it? — the mistress here! And she's got grandchildren! Even the old ones had stripped off!

3RD PEASANT. Oh lordy lordy me!

PRESENT COOK. So anyway, as soon as the music strikes up, the first thing that happens is that the gentlemen walk up to the ladies, put their arms round them, and away they go spinning.

2ND PEASANT. Even the old ladies?

PRESENT COOK. Even the old ladies.

SEMYON. No, the old ladies stay sat down.

PRESENT COOK. What are you talking about? I've seen it with my own eyes!

SEMYON. But that's not right,

OLD COOK (*hoarsely, leaning out from the stove*). The polka-mazurka! That's what you mean — the polka-mazurka! Eh, the fool, she doesn't know. Look, they dance it like this . . .

PRESENT COOK. Hold your tongue, you! Fine dancer you are! And there's somebody coming.

The OLD COOK *hurriedly conceals himself.*

Enter GRIGORY.

GRIGORY. Pickled cabbage.

PRESENT COOK. I've only just come up from the cellar. Now I've got to go running back. Who's it for?

GRIGORY. The young ladies. And sharp about it. Semyon can take it up — I'm busy.

PRESENT COOK. There they go, they stuff themselves with sweet things till they can stuff no more, then they long for something sharp.

1ST PEASANT. To clean out the system, like.

PRESENT COOK. Yes, and as soon as they've cleared a space they'll be off again!

Exit the PRESENT COOK, *taking a cup with her.*

GRIGORY (*to the* PEASANTS). Look at you sprawling here. You watch. If the mistress finds out she'll have the hide off you, just like she did this morning.

Exit GRIGORY.

1ST PEASANT. She certainly pitched in hot and strong this morning. Terrible, that was.

2ND PEASANT. *He* wanted to put his oar in, you could see. But then when he looked out and saw the way she was raising the roof he shut the door quick. If that's the way it is, says he to himself, then to hell with her.

3RD PEASANT. It's always the same story. Take my old woman.
She blazes up every now and then. A fearful sight. I'm away
out of the house before you can say knife. That's quite enough
of her! Just so much as look at her and she'll set about you
with the oven-tongs. Oh my lord!

    YAKOV *runs in with a prescription.*

YAKOV. Here, Semyon — run round to the chemist's, quick as
you can, and get these powders for the mistress.
SEMYON. But *he* told me not to go away.
YAKOV. You've got time. They won't do anything more now
till after they've got their tea out of the way . . . Sugar in your
tea.
1ST PEASANT. Sit down. Have a cup.

    Exit SEMYON.

YAKOV. I haven't got time for it, but all right, give me half a
cup, just so as I can keep you company.
1ST PEASANT. We were just talking about how high and mighty
the missus here came on this morning.
YAKOV. Oh, she's got a temper, that one. Terrible. Gets beside
herself with rage. Sometimes she even bursts into tears.
1ST PEASANT. Now what was it I wanted to ask you? Oh yes.
She kept going on this morning about *jarms.* Jarms, she says,
jarms! You've brought jarms with you! What might that have
been about, all that *jarms?*
YAKOV. Jarms? That wasn't jarms. That was jorms. What they
say is that there are these little insects, and off these little
insects, so they say, you get all the diseases. And they say
you've got these little insects on you. After you'd gone they
washed and washed away behind you, they sprayed and
sprayed away there where you'd been standing. There's a
special condiment that the little insects drink and then they
die of it.
2ND PEASANT. So where are they on us, then, these little
insects?
YAKOV (*drinks tea*). They say they're such teeny-weeny little
fellows you can't even see them with a glass.

2ND PEASANT. Then how does she know we've got them on us? There may be more of them on her than what there are on me.

YAKOV. I don't know. Go and ask *her*.

2ND PEASANT. I think it's all a lot of nonsense.

YAKOV. Everyone knows it's nonsense. The doctors have got to think something up, or what would anyone pay them money for? Round here every day he is, the doctor. Drives up, talks for a bit — ten roubles.

2ND PEASANT. Never!

YAKOV. Then there's another one that comes — a hundred roubles.

1ST PEASANT. A hundred roubles?

YAKOV. A hundred roubles, you say, a hundred roubles! If he was going out of town he'd want a thousand. A thousand roubles, he'd say, or you can croak.

3RD PEASANT. Oh my lord!

2ND PEASANT. What, he knows the magic word, does he?

YAKOV. He must do. I was in service once in the country, outside Moscow. With a general. Peppery old devil he was, proud as a tiger. Terrible! A real general! Well, he had a daughter, and this daughter she took sick. Straightaway they sent for this doctor fellow. 'A thousand roubles and I'll come.' Well, they agreed, and he came. But something upset him. And then, my word, lads, doesn't he just shut that general up! Oho, he says, so that's what you think of me, is it? Well, I won't treat her, then! So what can the old general do? He swallows his pride, and butters him up all ways on. 'My dear fellow! Anything, only don't throw up the case!'

1ST PEASANT. And they paid him the thousand?

YAKOV. What else?

2ND PEASANT. Easy money. What a peasant could do with that!

3RD PEASANT. I think it's all a lot of nonsense. Take me, now. I had footrot. I treated it, I treated it. Five roubles I treated my way through. I gave up treating it, and bless me if it didn't heal.

The OLD COOK *on the stove coughs.*

YAKOV. He's here again, is he, the poor soul?

1ST PEASANT. What manner of man is he?

YAKOV. He used to be the master's cook. Now he comes to see
   Lukerya — she's the cook here now.

1ST PEASANT. A chef, is he? So what, he stays here?

YAKOV. No, they won't have him here. He'll spend the day in
   one place, the night in another. Three kopecks in his pocket
   and he'll go to the doss-house. When he's drunk the lot he
   comes here.

2ND PEASANT. How did he get like that?

YAKOV. He just weakened. And once he was a man like the
   master. Went round with a gold watch in his pocket. Earned
   forty roubles a month. And now . . . well, if it hadn't been for
   Lukerya, he'd have died of hunger long since.

   Enter the PRESENT COOK, *with the pickled cabbage.*

YAKOV. I see he's here again.

PRESENT COOK. What do you want me to do with him — let
   him freeze?

3RD PEASANT. What drink can do to a man! (*Clicks his tongue
   in sympathy.*)

2ND PEASANT. Everyone knows — let a man take strength, and
   he's stronger than stone; let him weaken, and he's weaker than
   water.

OLD COOK (*crawls off the stove, his limbs shaking*). Lukerya!
   Give me a glass!

PRESENT COOK. Where are you off to? I'll give you a glass all
   right!

OLD COOK. Don't you walk in fear of God? I'm dying. Hey, lads,
   give us five kopecks.

PRESENT COOK. I'm telling you now — get back on the stove.

OLD COOK. Listen, cook — half-a-glass. For the love of Christ —
   do you understand? — I'm asking for it in the name of Christ!

PRESENT COOK. Come on, now. I'll give you tea instead.

OLD COOK. Tea? What's tea? It's a weak, empty drink. Some
   spirits, now. Just a mouthful . . . Lukerya!

3RD PEASANT. Oh, the poor soul, he's suffering such torments.

2ND PEASANT. Just give it to him, can't you?

PRESENT COOK (*gets the things from the dresser, and pours a
   glass*). There you are, then, and I'm giving you no more.

OLD COOK (*seizes it and drinks, shaking*). Lukerya! I'll drink it, yes, but what you've got to understand is this . . .

PRESENT COOK. Chatter, chatter! Just you get back on top of that stove, and not another sound out of you.

> The OLD COOK *climbs humbly back on to the stove, and continues to mutter something under his breath.*

2ND PEASANT. That's the way it is once a man's weakened.

1ST PEASANT. Weakness indeed is the nature of man.

3RD PEASANT. And that's the truth.

> The OLD COOK *lies down and continues to mutter. The others sit without speaking.*

2ND PEASANT. Well, now, what I wanted to ask you was — this girl from our part of the world who lives here — Aksinya's lass. What about her? What's she like? Is she a decent-living girl?

YAKOV. She's a good girl. Nothing but praise for her.

PRESENT COOK. I'm going to tell you straight, because I know from hard experience how things are in this town: if you want to take Tanya to be your son's wife, then take her as soon as you can, while she still hasn't been defiled, because there's no escaping it here.

YAKOV. Yes, that's true enough. Just last summer we had a girl living here called Natasha. A good girl. And then, for no reason at all, she fell. Fell as hard as him. (*Indicates the* OLD COOK.)

PRESENT COOK. You couldn't count how many girls of our sort in this town fall every day. They're lured by light work and sweet food. And as soon as they've caught sight of that, they're astray. And once they've gone astray they're not wanted any more. They're straightway turned off, and a new one takes their place. That's what happened with our Natasha. She went astray, and they put her out directly. She bore the child, she fell sick, and then last spring she died in hospital. And she was such a fine girl!

3RD PEASANT. Lord, lord! The people is weak. You can but take pity on them.

OLD COOK. Pity? You won't get pity from that lot, the swine!

(*Lowers his legs from the stove.*) Thirty years I roasted myself before their ovens. And as soon as I wasn't wanted, it's die, damn you! Die like a dog in the street! Pity? You'll get pity!

1ST PEASANT. Indeed, it's the old story, the old story.

2ND PEASANT. 'Here, boy! Here, Curly!'
                 All through the feast.
                 When nothing's left —
                 'Out, mangy beast!'

3RD PEASANT. Oh my lord!

OLD COOK. A lot you understand. What does this mean: *sauté à la Beaumont*? What's *bavaroise*? Oh, the things I could make! When you think the Emperor ate my handiwork! And now the swine don't want me. But I shan't knuckle under, not I!

PRESENT COOK. All right, you've had your say. Now I'm going to be after you! Back in your corner, so no one can see you, else old Fyodor or someone will come by, and they'll turn you out of the house and me along with you.

    Silence.

YAKOV. So you know my part of the world? Voznosenskoye?

2ND PEASANT. Of course we know it. Only a dozen miles from us, no more. Less if you go by the ford. What, you own land there, do you?

YAKOV. My brother owns the land — I send the money back. I may be here, but I'm dying for home.

1ST PEASANT. Indeed, indeed.

2ND PEASANT. Your brother would be Anisim, then, would he?

YAKOV. That's him. That's my brother. Far end from you.

2ND PEASANT. Right. Third house along.

    TANYA *runs in.*

TANYA. Yakov! What are you doing sitting about down here? She's calling!

YAKOV. I'm going. I'm going. What's up, then?

TANYA. Fifka's kicking up a shindy because Fifka wants her din-dins, and *she's* calling you all kinds of names. What a wicked man he is, she says. Utterly heartless, she says. It's long past her din-dins time, and that wicked man's still not bringing it!

YAKOV. Oh dear, in one of her tempers, is she? Here comes trouble.

PRESENT COOK. Take the pickled cabbage with you.

YAKOV. Give it here, then, give it here.

Exit YAKOV.

1ST PEASANT. Who's this now that's wanting their dinner?

TANYA. The dog. *Her* dog. (*Sits down and picks up the teapot.*) Any tea in the pot? If not I've brought some more. (*Puts it in.*)

2ND PEASANT. The *dog's* having dinner?

TANYA. Of course. They cook it a special cutlet, with not too much fat on it. And what do I do? — I wash the dog's underwear.

3RD PEASANT. Oh lordy lordy me!

TANYA. It's like the gentleman that gave his dog a funeral.

2ND PEASANT. How was that, then?

TANYA. It was like this, or so someone was telling me. There was this gentleman, and his dog went and died. So what did he do but he drove behind the dog's coffin in solemn procession to the graveyard. In the middle of winter. So all right, the dog's laid to rest and the funeral's over, and this gentleman's riding back in his carriage and he's weeping. Now, there's a good hard frost and the coachman's nose is running. (*Pours tea for the* PEASANTS.) So the coachman's nose keeps running, and the coachman keeps wiping it. The gentleman sees him. Hello, he says, what are you crying about? And the coachman says: Can't help but cry, sir, he was such a fine dog!

2ND PEASANT. And I'll wager all the time he's thinking: I'm damned if I'd cry even if you was to up and snuff it yourself!

OLD COOK (*from the stove*). Right. You've never said a truer word!

TANYA. All right, so the gentleman gets home, and straightway he says to his wife: what a good soul our coachman is, he says. He cried all the way home, he was so sorry for poor old Chum. Have him sent up. Here, he says to him, have a glass of vodka, and this is a small reward for you — one rouble.

The PEASANTS *laugh.*

1ST PEASANT. That's a beauty, that is!

2ND PEASANT. That's the way to do it!

3RD PEASANT. Ai, girl, you've made me laugh!

TANYA (*pours more tea*). Drink up! I don't know. Sometimes you get the feeling that life's all right. Other times it seems just disgusting, clearing up all their messes after them. Phhh! It's better in the country. Come on, drink up, and good health to you! I'll pour you another cup.

3RD PEASANT. Pour away, pour away.

1ST PEASANT. Well now, you clever lass, how's our business going?

TANYA. Don't worry. It's coming along.

1ST PEASANT. Semyon was saying . . .

TANYA (*quickly*). What was he saying?

2ND PEASANT. You couldn't make head nor foot of it, the way he told it.

TANYA. I can't tell you anything now, except that I'm doing my best, I'm doing my best. Here she is — your paper! (*Shows the paper, under her apron.*) If only this one little trick comes off! (*Squeals.*) Wouldn't it be beautiful?

2ND PEASANT. You watch out you don't lose the paper. That cost us money, too.

1ST PEASANT. Just do what you can for us to get the deal done, and we'll all give you away in marriage, the whole commune together.

TANYA. More tea.

3RD PEASANT. Just bring it off, now, and I'll come and dance at your wedding. Even though I've never in all my born days danced before!

TANYA (*laughs*). I'll live in hopes, then.

Silence.

2ND PEASANT (*inspecting* TANYA). Well, that's all as may be. But you're not fitted for a peasant's work.

TANYA. What, me? You think I've no strength in me, is that it?

You should see me lacing the mistress! There's plenty of
peasants that couldn't haul on her strings the way I haul on
them!

2ND PEASANT. Where do you haul her to?

TANYA. I haul her into a kind of thing made out of bones, like
a swan-off waistcoat. You heave away on the laces, and you
have to spit on your hands a few times, I can tell you, before
you've got her harnessed.

2ND PEASANT. You put the girth on her — saddle her up?

TANYA. I put the girth on her. Only I mayn't put my foot in her
flanks to do it.

2ND PEASANT. What does she want to be harnessed up for?

TANYA. She just does, that's all.

2ND PEASANT. Taken a vow, has she? Mortifying her flesh?

TANYA. No, it's to beautify her.

1ST PEASANT. She's hauling her belly out of the way. For the
look of the thing, like.

TANYA. You screw her tighter and tighter, till her eyes pop out
of her head, and still she says: More! I go on till my hands are
burning — and you say I've no strength in me!

The PEASANTS *laugh and shake their heads.*

But here am I chattering away when I've got work to do.

TANYA *runs out, laughing.*

3RD PEASANT. There's a girl for you! My, but she made me
laugh!

1ST PEASANT. She's so neat and tidy, though!

2ND PEASANT. That's all right. Don't you worry about her.

Enter VASILY *and* SAKHATOV, *the latter holding a
teaspoon.*

VASILY. But it wasn't exactly a dinner. It was a *déjeuner
dinatoir.* And a very dinnerish lunch it was, too. Leg of
sucking-pig — heavenly! They do you awfully well at Roulier's,
awfully well. In fact I've only just this moment got back.
(*Sees the* PEASANTS.) What? The peasantry here again?

SAKHATOV. Yes, yes, most interesting, but we've come here to hide the object. Now where can we put it?

VASILY. Excuse me one moment. (*To the* PRESENT COOK:) Where are the dogs, then?

PRESENT COOK. The dogs are in the coach-house. You didn't think they might have been put in *here,* did you?

VASILY. In the coach-house? Oh, that's all right.

SAKHATOV. I'm waiting.

VASILY. I'm frightfully sorry. What are we doing? We're hiding the spoon. Listen, I've an idea. One of these peasant chaps! Put it in his pocket. This one, say. (*To the* 3RD PEASANT.) Now listen to me. Are you listening? Where's your pocket?

3RD PEASANT. What do you want with my pocket? You get away from my pocket! I've got money in my pocket!

SAKHATOV. Where's his bag, then? They always have a bag or a bundle of some sort.

3RD PEASANT. What do you want with my bag?

PRESENT COOK. Speaking like that! This is the young master!

VASILY (*laughs*). You know why he's so scared? Because he's got tons and tons of money on him.

SAKHATOV. Yes, yes, I see. Anyway, this is what we'll do. You talk to them for a moment, while I slip the spoon into this bag of his without anyone noticing. If they don't know themselves where it is, there's no way they can indicate it to him. Go on, talk to them.

VASILY. Leave it to me. Well, then, chaps, are you buying that land, what?

1ST PEASANT. We're proposing to, with all our soul. But we're still not making headway.

VASILY. Don't you be so tight-fisted, then. Land — that's frightfully important stuff. I was telling you before — you want to grow mint. Or tobacco, that's another possibility.

1ST PEASANT. Indeed, any crops are possibilities.

3RD PEASANT. Young master, you ask your father for us. Else how are we to live?

SAKHATOV. *C'est fait.* All set. Off we go.

VASILY. So that's agreed, then. You're going to dip into that pocket of yours. Right? Bye bye, then.

Exeunt SAKHATOV *and* VASILY.

3RD PEASANT. I told you — we should have taken lodgings. Ten kopecks, say, and at least we'd have been left in peace. Lord help us in this place. Cough up your money, he says. What was all that about?

2ND PEASANT. He must have been drunk.

The PEASANTS *turn their cups over, stand up, and cross themselves.*

1ST PEASANT. Remember how he let that fall about sowing mint? You've got to make sense of that somehow.

2ND PEASANT. Sowing mint! Let him just try it. You bend yourself hump-backed! He'll be shouting for his mint all right! So thank you kindly, sir! Now then, lass, where are we going to sleep?

PRESENT COOK. One of you on the stove, the others on the benches.

3RD PEASANT. God save you. (*Prays.*)

1ST PEASANT. And God grant we finish our business. (*Lies down.*) By after dinner tomorrow we could be on the train. By Tuesday we could be home.

2ND PEASANT. Are you going to be putting out the light?

PRESENT COOK. Where, in here? Why, they'll be running in and out all the time, one after another. I'll turn it down a bit, though. Just you put your feet up, now.

2ND PEASANT. How do you live on small plots like ours? I've been buying bread since Christmas. Now I've come to the end of my oat straw. If I could just put my hands on ten or twelve acres, I'd take Semyon home.

1ST PEASANT. Yes, for you it's a family matter into the bargain. But never you fear. You'll harvest that land yet, if only we can get our business done.

3RD PEASANT. We must pray to Our Lady in Heaven. Maybe she'll take pity.

Silence. Breathing. Then there is a tramp of feet and the sound of voices, and the doors are flung wide open. In rush headlong: GROSSMANN, *blindfold and holding* SAKHATOV *by the hand; the* PROFESSOR *and the* DOCTOR; *the* STOUT LADY *and the* MASTER; BETSY

and PETRISCHEV; VASILY *and* MARYA; *the*
MISTRESS *and the* COUNTESS; FYODOR *and* TANYA.
The PEASANTS *start up.*
GROSSMANN, *after his rapid entry, comes to a stop.*

STOUT LADY. Don't worry, everyone, I've got my eye on him.
I took the job on, and I'm carrying out my duties very strictly!
You're not leading him, are you?

SAKHATOV. Certainly not.

STOUT LADY. Don't lead him — but don't hold him back,
either. (*To the* MASTER:) I know what these experiments are
like. I've done them myself. In my case, I usually feel a sort of
flowing forth, and as soon as I feel the *flowing forth,* then I
know . . .

MASTER. May I please ask you to observe silence?

STOUT LADY. Of course, I completely understand! I've
experienced exactly the same thing with myself. As soon as
my attention is distracted, I can't feel the *flowing* . . .

MASTER. Sh!

They move along, searching round the 1ST *and* 2ND
PEASANTS, *and then reach the* 3RD. GROSSMANN
stumbles against the bench.

COUNTESS (*to* MISTRESS). *Mais dites-moi.* (*Aside.*) Is he
getting paid for this?

MISTRESS. I couldn't tell you.

COUNTESS. But he's a gentleman, is he?

MISTRESS. Oh yes.

COUNTESS. *Ça tient du miraculeux. N'est ce pas?* How does he
do it?

MISTRESS. *Je ne saurais vous dire.* My husband will explain it
to you. (*Sees the* PEASANTS.) *Pardon* . . .

The COUNTESS *joins the others.*

(*To the* PRESENT COOK:) What's this? Who let them in?

PRESENT COOK. Yakov brought them in.

MISTRESS. Yakov? And who told Yakov to bring them in?

PRESENT COOK. That I don't know. But Fyodor saw them here.

MISTRESS (*to the* MASTER). Leonid!

MASTER (*absorbed in the search*). Sh!

MISTRESS. Fyodor! What is the meaning of this? Didn't you see
me disinfecting the room they were in before? And now you've
infected the whole kitchen for me! All the food! All the
drink!

FYODOR. I didn't think it would be dangerous in here. They are
away on business, after all. They are a long way from their own
part of the country.

MISTRESS. That's just the trouble! They're from Kursk, where
people are dying like flies from diphtheria! But what chiefly
concerns me is that I gave orders they were to be kept out of
the house! Did I or did I not give those orders? (*Goes up to the
group of people gathered round the* PEASANTS.) Take care!
Don't touch them! They're all infectious! They've all got
diphtheria!

> *No one listens to her. She turns aside, on her dignity, and
> stands waiting.*

PETRISHCHEV (*sniffs loudly*). I don't know about infection,
but they're certainly rather an infliction. Can you smell?

BETSY. You do talk nonsense, don't you! Vovo, which bag is it
in?

VASILY. That one, that one! He's getting warmer, he's getting
warmer!

PETRISHCHEV. What is the mysterious power in this room —
a ghostly spell or a ghastly smell?

BETSY. This is where your cigarettes are rather handy. Come on,
now — smoke away — Closer to me!

> PETRISHCHEV *leans towards her and fumigates the air.*

VASILY. He's getting there, look!

GROSSMANN (*fumbles anxiously around the* 3RD PEASANT).
Here! I feel it's somewhere here!

STOUT LADY. Do you feel a *flowing forth*?

> GROSSMANN *bends down over the bag and brings out the
> spoon.*

OMNES. Bravo!

General delight.

VASILY. What? So that's where our spoon had got to! (*To the* 3RD PEASANT:) That's the sort of thing you get up to, is it?

3RD PEASANT. What do you mean, get up to? I never took your spoon! What's he mixing me up in it for? I never took it and I never took it and my soul knows I never did! Look at him, not me! I could see he was up to no good. Give me your purse, he says. I never took it! As Christ's my witness I never took it!

The young people cluster round him and laugh.

MASTER (*to his son, angrily*). Forever up to some idiocy! (*To the* 3RD PEASANT:) Don't upset yourself, my friend. We know you didn't take it. It was merely an experiment.

GROSSMANN (*takes off the blindfold and gives the appearance of having just woken up*). If I might trouble you for some . . . water.

They all fuss round him.

VASILY. Anyway, let's all go over to the coach-house, what? I'll show you a certain little bow-wow I've got out there. Stunning little beast!

BETSY. 'Bow-wow' — what a repulsive way of talking about it! Why can't you say 'dog?'

VASILY. Because I can't. Supposing I said 'What a stunning little human being Betsy is!' No, I've got to say, 'What a stunning little filly!' Isn't that right, Marya? (*Laughs.*)

MARYA. Come on, then.

Exeunt MARYA, BETSY, PETRISHCHEV *and* VASILY.

STOUT LADY (*to* GROSSMANN). Well? How is it? Are you recovered?

GROSSMANN *doesn't answer.*

STOUT LADY (*to* SAKHATOV). What about you? Did you feel a flowing forth?

SAKHATOV. I didn't feel anything. But that was excellent,

excellent. Completely successful.

BARONESS *C'était admirable!* It doesn't hurt him, does it?

MASTER. *Pas le moins du monde.* Not in the slightest.

PROFESSOR. Would you oblige us, doctor?

DOCTOR. Professor?

PROFESSOR. His temperature.

DOCTOR. Certainly, professor.

PROFESSOR. At the start of the experiment it was 98.9. I think that's right? And would you be good enough to check his pulse as well? Some expenditure of energy must inevitably have occurred.

DOCTOR (*to* GROSSMANN). If you would be so kind, sir. (*Administers the thermometer and takes his wrist.*)

STOUT LADY. May I be permitted to ask — could the state you were in be described as sleep?

GROSSMANN (*wearily*). The same as before — hypnosis.

SAKHATOV. So we are to understand that you hypnotised yourself?

GROSSMANN. Why not? Hypnosis can be induced not only by association — as for example Charcot does, by the sound of a tom-tom — but also merely by entering a hypnogenetic zone.

SAKHATOV. Let us accept that this is the case. But would it not be desirable all the same to define a little more precisely just what hypnosis is?

PROFESSOR. Hypnosis is a phenomenon in which one form of energy is converted into another.

GROSSMANN. Charcot does not define it like that.

SAKHATOV. It may be your definition, professor, but if I may say so, when I was talking to Liébault — who is after all one of the world's authorities on the subject — *he* told me . . .

STOUT LADY. No, if I may say so, I agree with the professor here. And I have the best possible evidence. Because when I was lying in bed unconscious after my illness, I was suddenly seized by a compulsion to talk. Now usually I'm rather a silent person, but here suddenly was this compulsion to talk and talk. They told me afterwards that everyone was simply amazed at the way I'd talked. (*To* SAKHATOV). I'm sorry — I believe I interrupted you.

SAKHATOV. Not at all. Please go on.

DOCTOR. Pulse 82, and the temperature has risen by half a point.

PROFESSOR. Well, there's your proof for you! Just what should
    have happened. (*Takes out a notebook and writes.*) 82, yes?
    And 99.4? As soon as hypnosis is induced, we always observe
    an increase in the activity of the heart.

DOCTOR. I can testify as a doctor that your prediction has been
    completely fulfilled.

MASTER. So what do you think, then? Should we risk a full-
    scale seance with our new medium?

PROFESSOR. Certainly. He is undoubtedly a powerful one. The
    main thing is that we should do it as soon as possible and with
    the same participants. Grossmann should undoubtedly respond
    to the influence of psychic energy. The connections between
    hypnotic and psychic phenomena — their underlying unity —
    will thus be still more evident. You will see that if the medium
    is as powerful as he was today, Grossmann will begin to vibrate
    in sympathy.

MASTER. Tomorrow, then, without fail.

PROFESSOR. Saturday. Isn't that the day when your charming
    wife receives?

MASTER. So much the better. We shall shut ourselves up in my
    study and be quite undisturbed. Now, let us go back into the
    house. (*Ushers everyone towards the door.*)

SAKHATOV. I was merely going to say that when I was talking
    to Liébault, he told me that hypnosis was nothing more than a
    special psychic condition that increases suggestibility.

PROFESSOR. Perfectly true. But the main thing nonetheless
    is the physical Law of Equivalence.

GROSSMANN. Besides, Liébault is far from being an authority
    — whereas Charcot has carried out the most thorough
    investigation and demonstrated that when hypnosis is produced
    by a blow, or in trauma . . .

MASTER (*at the door*). Countess, please!

SAKHATOV. I am not for one moment denying Charcot's work.
    I know Charcot as well. I am merely repeating what Liébault
    told me . . .

GROSSMANN. There are 3,000 patients in the Salpétrière, where

Charcot works, and I have attended the entire course of his lectures . . .

PROFESSOR. Excuse me, gentlemen, excuse me — that is not the point . . .

STOUT LADY. I can explain it all in two words. When my husband was ill, the doctors all simply gave up . . . .

> *Exeunt the* COUNTESS, SAKHATOV, *the* PROFESSOR, GROSSMANN, *the* DOCTOR, *and the* STOUT LADY, *all talking at once and interrupting each other. The* MISTRESS *catches the* MASTER *by the sleeve and detains him.*

MISTRESS. How many times have I begged you not to interfere in the running of the house! You don't know about anything outside all that rubbish of yours, and the house is my business. You'll have everyone infected!

MASTER. Who? What? Me? I don't know what on earth you're talking about!

MISTRESS. What do you mean, you don't know what I'm talking about? There are people with diphtheria camping out in the kitchen here! And there's a perpetual to-and-fro between the kitchen and the house!

MASTER. Yes, but I don't know . . .

MISTRESS. 'I don't know'! Don't know what?

MASTER. Anything about it.

MISTRESS. But you *ought* to know, if you're the head of the household! You mustn't do things like this!

MASTER. But I didn't think . . . I just thought . . . Or rather . . .

MISTRESS. I can't bear to listen to you! (*To* FYODOR:) Get them out of my kitchen at once! It's appalling. No one does what they're told. They're always just trying to spite me. I drive them out of *there*, and at once people let them in *here*. (*Gets more and more agitated, and closer and closer to tears.*) It's just to spite me! Just to spite me! And I'm a sick woman . . . ! Doctor! Doctor! Where is he? Even he's gone off and left me. (*Sobs.*)

> *Exit the* MISTRESS, *with the* MASTER *after her.*

> *Tableau. Everyone stands for a long time in silence.*

3RD PEASANT. Well, God save them, the lot of them. If you so much as look at anyone in this place you'll end up in the police-station. And I've never been in trouble in my life. Come on, lads, let's go and find some lodgings.

FYODOR (*to* TANYA). Where can they go, then?

TANYA. Don't worry — we'll put them in the coach-house.

FYODOR. How in the coach-house, when the coachman's just been complaining it's full of dogs?

TANYA. All right, then — in the yardman's lodge.

FYODOR. But what if she finds out?

TANYA. She won't find out. Don't fuss now. We can't turn them out in the night, can we? They won't find anything now.

FYODOR. Well, you do as you think best. Just so long they're not here.

>*Exit* FYODOR.
>*The* PEASANTS *gather up their bags.*

OLD COOK. The damned swine! Live like a hog, die mad as a dog — that's them! The swine!

PRESENT COOK. Quiet you. Just thank the lord they didn't see you.

TANYA. Off we go, then, my dears. Off to the yardman's lodge.

1ST PEASANT. But what about our business? How are we with regard to his putting his hand to it and signing? Can we live in hopes?

TANYA. That we'll know tomorrow.

2ND PEASANT. You're going to outwit him?

TANYA (*laughs*). God willing, I am!

>*Curtain.*

Act Three

The same as Act One.

FYODOR, GRIGORY, *and two liveried* GROOMS; *one of them, the* COUNTESS's, *with grey sidewhiskers.*

COUNTESS'S GROOM. You're the third lot we've called on today. Thanks be to God that all the ladies with calling days live in the same part of town. You used to have yours on Thursdays, didn't you?

FYODOR. Then they changed it to Saturday, so it was the same as the Golovkins and the Grade von Grabes, and all the rest of them.

SILENT GENTLEMAN'S GROOM. They look after us grooms all right at the Shcherbakovs', I can tell you — just like there was a ball every week.

Enter YAKOV *from the living room door at the top of the stairs, carrying a tray of dirty crockery. He hurries down the stairs.*

YAKOV. Whew! (*To* FYODOR:) You might tell Grigory to give me a hand up there. I can't cope with these afternoons of hers all on my own.

Exit YAKOV *into the pantry.*

COUNTESS'S GROOM. You've got a hard-working one there.

FYODOR. Oh, he's a good lad. (*To* GRIGORY:) Go on, then. Give him a hand. I'll look after things down here. He can't manage by himself.

GRIGORY. He's just cack-handed. That's why he can't manage. (*Exit* GRIGORY *upstairs.*)

Enter the MASTER *from his study.*

MASTER (*to* FYODOR). The Professor. Has the Professor arrived yet?

Enter the PROFESSOR *upstairs.*

PROFESSOR. Are we ready, then?

MASTER. Ah, Professor!

PROFESSOR. I felt myself in duty bound to pay my respects to your charming wife first of all.

MASTER. Of course. Of course.

PROFESSOR. I must confess that I am looking forward to our seance with the keenest interest.

MASTER. I think we might commence just as soon as we can extricate the Doctor and Mr. Grossmann from my wife's clutches. If we can manage to do that without attracting too much attention. In principle, of course, I believe that our little experiments should be open to all, including the unbelievers and the scoffers . . .

PROFESSOR. Indeed, indeed.

MASTER. But today, with a new and untried medium, I feel that perhaps . . .

PROFESSOR. Quite, quite.

Enter SAKHATOV *at the top of the stairs.*

SAKHATOV. Ah! Your wife and some of the others have sat down to cards. Since I am left over . . . There is to be a seance, is there?

MASTER. Oh . . . yes, yes. We were of course hoping that you would be able to . . .

SAKHATOV. With your new medium?

PROFESSOR. If our preliminary experiment yesterday was a true guide, I believe he will prove to be quite remarkably powerful.

MASTER. In the servants' hall, apparently, they noticed it a long time ago. He will sit down to table, and the spoon will jump into his hand of its own accord. (*To the* PROFESSOR:) Did you hear about that?

PROFESSOR. That, I have to confess, I had not heard.

SAKHATOV (*to the* PROFESSOR). But nonetheless you admit the possibility of such phenomena?

PROFESSOR. Of which phenomena?

SAKHATOV. Well, of spiritualistic, psychic phenomena in general. Of supernatural phenomena.

PROFESSOR. It depends upon what we call supernatural . . .
MASTER. Perhaps we should try to find Grossmann and the
Doctor before anyone else emerges.

Enter YAKOV *from the pantry, carrying a tray with tea
and pastries. He hurries upstairs.*

I should explain — we felt that it would be better to limit our
numbers to those with a more serious interest in the subject.
Such as yourself. Oh, Yakov! One moment.

YAKOV *runs back downstairs.*

Ask the Doctor and Mr. Grossmann to join the Professor and
myself in the study, will you? Tell them we are ready to
commence.

YAKOV *runs back upstairs and goes off.*

PROFESSOR (*to* SAKHATOV). When a nail was first attracted,
not by a living person, but by a piece of stone — how did this
phenomenon strike observers — as natural or as supernatural?
SAKHATOV. Yes, yes, yes. Only phenomena such as magnetic
attraction can be constantly repeated.
PROFESSOR. And it is exactly the same here. The phenomenon
is repeated, and we confirm it by investigation. Moreover we
subsume the phenomena we have investigated under laws that
are common also to other phenomena . . .

Exeunt the MASTER, *the* PROFESSOR, *and* SAKHATOV,
into the study.

FYODOR. No, he's a good lad, is Yakov, but the mistress don't
like him. Don't look presentable, she says. And then yesterday
they were going on about him because he let the peasants
into the kitchen. It's a wonder they didn't sack him. But he's
a good lad.
SILENT GENTLEMAN'S GROOM. What peasants were these?
FYODOR. They'd come up from our Kursk estate to buy some
land. Anyway, he took them through into the kitchen, and
the mistress found them. My word, there was trouble! What,
she says, people who may be infectious, and you let them into

the kitchen? She's very frightened of this infection business.

COUNTESS'S GROOM. All these infections! What kind of latest
fashion is this, then? Yours is afraid of them, too, is she?

FYODOR. More frightened of infections than the house burning
down. All we do now is rush about fumigating and washing
and spraying.

COUNTESS'S GROOM. So that's the fearful smell I can smell.

YAKOV *runs downstairs.*

FYODOR. Now what?

YAKOV. No bread and butter! I told them . . .

YAKOV *runs into the pantry.*

COUNTESS'S GROOM. It's beyond everything, the sins that are
committeed over these infections. A real bad business! People
forget God, even. Our master's sister, Princess Mosolova — her
little daughter was dying. And what happened? They never
went into the room — not her father nor her mother neither.
They never took their leave of her. The little girl was crying
and calling for them. And they never went in. The doctor
had found some infection or other. The maid and the nurse —
they were in and out to her all the time, and they were all right,
they survived.

SILENT GENTLEMAN'S GROOM. Or take my people. The
young master fell sick. So straightway they carted him off with
a nurse, and put him in a hotel. And there he died, without
his mother.

COUNTESS'S GROOM. Sin? — It doesn't frighten *them*. But
you'll never get away from God, that's my belief.

FYODOR. That's my belief, too.

YAKOV *runs in from the pantry with bread and butter,
and goes upstairs. Enter the* MASTER *from his study.*

MASTER. Yakov!

YAKOV. Yes! Yes! I'll tell them now.

Exeunt the MASTER *into his study, and* YAKOV *upstairs.*

COUNTESS'S GROOM. And bear this in mind: they may not

fear sin, they may not fear God, but they're so afraid of each other they have to lock themselves up within four walls, just as if they was in prison.

The PRINCESS *and her* DAUGHTER *come downstairs, being seen out by* BETSY, *who is followed by* GRIGORY.

PRINCESS. So tell your Papa that I don't believe a *word.* But all the same I'll come and have a look at this new medium of his. Just let him tell me when.

She sits down on the settle, and looks at her visiting book and her watch. GRIGORY *puts her boots on.*

PRINCESS'S DAUGHTER. And please — *do* come this evening. If you decline, then Dodo will, too, and we shall get nowhere at all.

BETSY. I don't know. I absolutely *must* go to the Shubins. Then I've got the rehearsal.

DAUGHTER. You can fit us in. No, *please!* You mustn't let us down. Fedya's going to be there, and Coco, too.

BETSY. Coco? I've had absolutely as much as I can stand of your Coco.

DAUGHTER. I thought I'd find him here. *Ordinairement il est d'une exactitude . . .*

BETSY. Oh, he'll certainly be coming.

DAUGHTER. Whenever I see the two of you together it always looks as though either he's just that moment proposed or he's just the next moment going to.

BETSY. Yes, I shall probably have to go through it sooner or later. So awful!

DAUGHTER. Poor Coco! So in love!

BETSY. *Cessez — les gens.*

The PRINCESS'S DAUGHTER *sits down on the little sofa, and converses in a whisper.* GRIGORY *puts her boots on.*

DAUGHTER. Until this evening, then.

BETSY. I'll try.

PRINCESS. So just let your Papa tell me when. *Au revoir,* then, you lovely creature.

Kisses her, and goes out with her DAUGHTER. BETSY
goes back upstairs.

GRIGORY. I hate putting an old trout like that into her boots.
They can't bend — they can't see over their stomachs — they
keep shoving their foot everywhere except where it's supposed
to go. It's another matter with the young one. Taking her
little foot in your hands — that's nice.

SILENT GENTLEMAN'S GROOM. Oh, he picks and chooses,
doesn't he?

COUNTESS'S GROOM. It's not for the likes of us to pick and
choose over the likes of them.

GRIGORY. Why not? We're people, aren't we? It's them that
think we understand nothing. When they were talking just
back then, they looked up at me — and straightway: *'Les gens!'*

SILENT GENTLEMAN'S GROOM. What's that, then?

GRIGORY. In plain language that means: Don't talk — they'll
take it in. It's the same at the dinner-table. But I can understand them all right. You talk about the difference between
us and them — there's no difference.

COUNTESS'S GROOM. There's a great difference, for them that
understand it.

GRIGORY. There's no difference. Today I'm a footman. But
tomorrow, who knows, maybe I'll be living as good as them.
Sometimes they even get married to footmen. It's happened,
hasn't it? Well, I'm going for a smoke.

FYODOR. No, you go back up there and help Yakov.

Exit GRIGORY *upstairs.*

SILENT GENTLEMAN'S GROOM. He's a bold one, all right.

FYODOR. He's an idle lad. Not fitted for service. Used to be a
clerk, and that spoiled him. I didn't recommend taking him
on, but the mistress liked him. He looks presentable when she
goes out driving.

COUNTESS'S GROOM. I'd like to see him up against our master.
The count'd give him what for, and no mistake. He's no love
for restless souls like that. You're a footman, all right, so be a
footman. Show you've a right to the title. All this pride — it's
not fitting.

Enter the MASTER *from the study.*

MASTER. What can that silly Yakov be doing? I suppose I shall have to go up there myself.

> *The* MISTRESS *enters at the top of the stairs, seeing out an elderly* COUNTESS *with false teeth and a wig. They are attended by* GRIGORY.

Oh.

MISTRESS. Of course I shall, of course. I shall of course be there.

> *Exit the* MASTER *into the study.*

I'm so touched that you took the trouble today.

COUNTESS. I should be here more often if it were not for my health.

MISTRESS. Really, you must go to this man I have . . .

> *Enter* YAKOV. *He runs down the stairs.*

YAKOV. Oranges! And another samovar!

FYODOR. Just ask the housekeeper.

> YAKOV *runs into the pantry.* GRIGORY *helps the* COUNTESS *into her overcoat and boots.*

MISTRESS. This man of mine — you must try him. He's a trifle bluntly spoken, but no one can set your mind at rest the way he can. He makes everything so clear and simple.

COUNTESS. No, no, I've got used to my man now.

MISTRESS. Look after yourself, won't you?

> YAKOV *runs in from the pantry.*

YAKOV. We haven't got many oranges.

FYODOR. Just give them what we have. Here, let me look.

> *Exeunt* YAKOV *and* FYODOR *into the pantry.*

COUNTESS. *Merci, mille fois merci.*

MISTRESS. *Ma chère contesse, c'est moi qui vous remercie.*

COUNTESS. Until Tuesday, then.

Exeunt the COUNTESS *and her* GROOM. YAKOV *runs in from the pantry, intent upon the full samovar and the bowl of oranges he is carrying. He runs in front of the* MISTRESS *up the stairs, dropping oranges.*

MISTRESS. Yakov! Do you do it just to annoy me?

The MISTRESS *goes upstairs.*
YAKOV *runs back down the stairs with the samovar and bowl, recovering the oranges he has dropped.* GRIGORY *watches him.*

YAKOV. Oh dear. Oh dear oh dear oh dear.

Exit the MISTRESS.
Enter the MASTER *from the study.*

MASTER (*to* YAKOV). What are you doing? Where have you been? Have you told them?
YAKOV. I was just . . . I just had to . . . I was just going to . . . I'll do it now. (*Exit* YAKOV *upstairs.*)

Exit GRIGORY *into the pantry.*
Enter SAKHATOV *and the* PROFESSOR *from the study.*

PROFESSOR (*to* SAKHATOV). But this is false!
SAKHATOV. Not at all. The phenomena, or so we are told, are produced by certain particular individuals.
PROFESSOR. But this is false!
SAKHATOV (*to the* MASTER). Have you found them?
MASTER. I don't know what that butler of mine does with himself. He doesn't seem to realise that some of us are busy people.
PROFESSOR. The phenomena are produced not by the medium, but by spiritual energy acting through the medium; and this is a great difference.

Enter PETRISHCHEV *upstairs.*

PETRISHCHEV. All right, then. My first rhymes with pay, and my second with pack.
MASTER. Oh, not him. Above all not him. Perhaps we should withdraw into the study.

The MASTER *ushers* SAKHATOV *and the* PROFESSOR
back into his study.

PETRISHCHEV. And my whole is a thing . . . Oh.

Enter YAKOV *upstairs.*

YAKOV (*to* PETRISHCHEV). In the study, he wants you in the
   study.
PETRISHCHEV. In the study, certainly. Listen to this . . .
YAKOV. It's for the spirits.
PETRISHCHEV. Listen — my first rhymes with pay, and my
   second with pack . . . I wish you wouldn't keep looking over
   your shoulder like that.

   Enter, through the front door, COCO KLINGEN, *wearing
   pince-nez.*

   Coco! My dear old Coco-Bloko! I think you're just in time to
   raise some spirits. You've raised mine already. Where have
   you sprung from?

   Exit YAKOV, *upstairs.*

COCO. From the Shcherbakovs'. What are you doing? Up to your
   idiotic games, as usual?
PETRISHCHEV. No, listen, it's a riddle. My first syllable rhymes
   with pay, my second with pack, and my whole is a thing you
   keep needles in.
COCO. I've no idea. And I've no time, either.
PETRISHCHEV. Why, where do you still have to get to?
COCO. What do you mean, where? I have to be at the Ivins', for
   choir practice. Then I have to go to the Shubins', and then to
   the rehearsal. I take it you have to be at that, too, don't you?
PETRISHCHEV. Absolutely. Rehearsing away until that poor
   old hearse is as good as new. First of all I was playing a savage.
   Now I'm playing a savage and a general.
COCO. Anyway, how did the hypnotic session go last night?
PETRISHCHEV. Oh, it was hilarious. We played hunt-the-spoon
   in the servants' kitchen, and it was full of smelly peasants, and
   Vovo gave one poor old smelly peasant the fright of his life.

'So this is where our spoon is!' says Vovo. 'I never done it!'
says the poor smelly old fellow. 'And remember I be an
orphan and me not eighty yet.' Oh, it was tremendous fun!
Frightful shame you weren't there.

COCO. I'm rather afraid of you, *mon cher*. You manage to reduce
it all to a string of jokes. I can't help feeling that if I so much
as say a word to you, it will be twisted, and I'll find I've gone
down on my knees to her and made a complete proposal. And
that wouldn't suit me at all.

PETRISHCHEV. All right, then, you propose, and I'll speak against
the motion. Then we'll adjourn, and the vital question will
never even be put to the vote. Why don't you look in on Vovo?
There's hours before we have to go off and rehorse the hearse.

COCO. I don't understand how you can associate with such an
idiot as Vovo. He's so stupid — he really is a hopeless case.

PETRISHCHEV. Oh, I love him! I suppose he's a rather odd taste.
But there's going to be a seance in a minute, and you'll see
Vovo absolutely at his best. (*Exit* PETRISHCHEV *into*
VASILY's *room*.)

> *Enter* BETSY *down the stairs, seeing a* LADY *out*.
> COCO *bows markedly*. BETSY *shakes hands with him*.

BETSY. Hello. Do you know each other?

LADY. I don't think . . .

BETSY. Baron Klingen. Why weren't you here yesterday?

COCO. I simply couldn't manage the time.

BETSY. What a shame. It was very interesting. Tell me, is our
charade progressing?

COCO. Indeed it is. The verses for my second syllable are done.
Nicky wrote them, and I composed the music.

BETSY. How do they go? Tell me.

COCO. What is it, now? Oh, yes. The knight is singing to Deedee.
Deedee is the name of his lady love. (*Sings*.)
O Deedee, dealer in delight,
Deem thou me worthy of thy sight.
Mine eyes devour thee day and night,
O Deedee, Deedee, dee dee dee!

LADY. Dee!

COCO. You're absolutely right. That's my second syllable. My
   first syllable is Mala.

BETSY. Mala is the name of a cannibal princess. She always
   wants to eat the object of her love. So as she walks along,
   suffering all the pangs of passion, she sings:
>   For love I pine —

COCO. It's half-past nine —

BETSY. And I have had no dinner.
>   Who'll be the meal
>   For which I feel
>   Such hopeless longing simmer?

COCO. Then lo! a moat!
>   And there's a boat!
>   With two full generals in her!

BETSY. But which to eat?
>   They're both so sweet!
>   Which lucky man will win her?

BETSY & COCO (*together*).
>   She sits and sighs —
>   She starves — she dies.
>   How cruel love's dilemma!

LADY. *Charmant!*

BETSY. You see what nonsense it is.

COCO. But that's the beauty of it!

LADY. And who is playing the cannibal princess?

BETSY. I am, and I had the costume made, but Mama says it's
   indecent. It's no more indecent than what she wears to a ball.
   (*To* FYODOR). Have they come from Bourdet's?

FYODOR. Yes — he's waiting in the kitchen this time.

LADY. So how are you doing the whole word?

BETSY. You'll see. I don't want to spoil the surprise. *Au revoir.*

LADY. Goodbye. (*Exit the* LADY.)

BETSY (*to* COCO). Come and see Mama.

> *Exeunt* BETSY *and* COCO *upstairs. Enter* VASILY *and*
> PETRISHCHEV, *smoking* papirosy, *from* VASILY's *room.*

VASILY. But he's such an absolute numskull, your Coco-Bloko.
   I can't stand him. Just gads about. Nothing to do except
   polish ballroom floors.

PETRISHCHEV. All right, then — no Coco-Bloko. Off we go.

They put on their overcoats.

VASILY. First of all we'll just take a look at the dogs, in the
coach-house. You know, one of those little bow-wows is so
fierce the coachman says he almost ate him.
PETRISHCHEV. The coachman? Ate the dog?
VASILY. Oh, you and your jokes!

Enter the MASTER, SAKHATOV *and the* PROFESSOR
from the study. VASILY *and* PETRISHCHEV *stop at the
sight of them.*

PROFESSOR. But the point is, that the whole transaction is
governed by a law of physics — the Law of Equivalence . . .

Enter, upstairs, the STOUT LADY.

STOUT LADY. Your wife has kindly dispensed with me, so that
I might come and join your party.
MASTER. Oh. Please.
STOUT LADY. I think Grossmann has recovered. He was
absolutely exhausted yesterday. He could scarcely hold a
teacup. You noticed the way he went pale the moment he got
near the object? I noticed it at once. I remarked upon it
before anyone else.
PROFESSOR. Undoubtedly, a loss of vital energy.
STOUT LADY. And what I'm saying is that this kind of thing
must not be abused. Because someone I know once went to a
hypnotist — this was Verochka Konshina — but of course you
know here — and he's hypnotised her into giving up smoking —
and at once she had trouble with her back instead.
MASTER. Shall we retire into the study, then?
STOUT LADY. If I might just finish. So I said to her, I said, 'It's
better to smoke than suffer with your nerves like that.' Of
course, smoking is bad for you, and I should like to give it up
myself, but what can I do? — I can't do it! Once I didn't
smoke for a whole fortnight, but then I simply couldn't hold
out for another minute.
MASTER. We are almost ready to begin . . .

STOUT LADY. Oh, we must tell the others, then. (*Turns back from the study, and begins to move upstairs.*) Now, you were talking about a loss of strength . . .
MASTER. No, no.
PROFESSOR. Wait.
SAKHATOV. One moment.

The MASTER, *the* PROFESSOR, *and* SAKHATOV
follow her up the stairs, trying to halt the flow.

STOUT LADY. I was merely going to say that in the days when I used to travel about by post-chaise — the roads then were appalling — you wouldn't remember this, but it's something I always used to remark upon, and I can tell you that whatever you may say, all our nervous trouble today comes from the railways . . .
MASTER. Before we go any further . . .
STOUT LADY (*to* VASILY *and* PETRISHCHEV). The seance! Don't forget the seance!

VASILY *and* PETRISHCHEV *take off their overcoats and follow the* STOUT LADY's *party upstairs.*

MASTER. If I might say one word . . .
STOUT LADY. Yes, yes, but take me, for example. Now, I can never sleep while I'm travelling. I'll go one night without sleep — two nights — three nights — and *still* I can't get off! You could kill me and I shouldn't get to sleep!

Exeunt the MASTER, *the* PROFESSOR, SAKHATOV,
the STOUT LADY, VASILY, *and* PETRISHCHEV.
Enter TANYA *from the pantry. She crosses to the*
MASTER's *study, then stops and looks round. She opens the door a crack and looks inside.*
Enter FYODOR *from the pantry, carrying some albums.*

FYODOR. What are you doing here?
TANYA. I want a word with you.
FYODOR. What about?
TANYA. There's one more thing I want to ask you to do for me.
FYODOR. What is it now?

TANYA. Is this where the seance is to be?

FYODOR. It always is.

TANYA. If he does sign the paper, and Semyon can go home with his father, and we can get married — will you ask her to let me leave? My life's not here any more.

Enter YAKOV. *He runs down the stairs and off into the pantry.*

FYODOR. A fine time you've picked. You can see what a hustle and bustle we're in.

TANYA. But you know better than anyone — there'll be no end to hustle and bustle, however long we wait. And what I'm taking on now is going to last all my life long. You've been so good to me already. Be my own father for me again. Pick the right moment and tell her. Because if she flies up she won't give me my papers.

FYODOR. But why are you in such a state about it?

TANYA. Why, because if he once signs that paper I'd like to be off to my godmother and get everything ready. We could be married the week after Easter. If he signs that paper.

FYODOR. All right, then. Now, I've got work to do . . . But are they really and truly going to sit Semyon down with them?

TANYA. Apparently. After all, they've already sat him down with them once.

FYODOR. Well, it beats me. (*Puts on his pince-nez.*) Is he clean?

TANYA. How should I know?

FYODOR. So here's what you do. You go and fetch the nailbrush and the soap — the good soap — from my room, if you like — and you cut his claws and wash him clean as an apple.

TANYA. He can wash himself.

FYODOR. Well, you just tell him, then. And tell him to put on clean shirt and underclothes.

TANYA. Right.

Exit TANYA *into the pantry.*

FYODOR (*alone. Opens one of the albums he is carrying*). This is their spirit photographs. Look at this one — the master with the materialisation of a Turkish gentleman. A wondrous thing is human weakness. I wonder if they've got their accordion and guitar laid out this time for all those departed souls to give them a tune on.

Enter MASTER *down the stairs.*

MASTER. Well, then, are we all ready?

FYODOR. We are. Only I don't know whether your new medium might not let you down with your friends.

MASTER. No, the Professor and I tried him out yesterday. He's a remarkably powerful one.

FYODOR. I wouldn't know about that. Only, is he clean? You never thought to tell him to wash his hands. It could be a little awkward, all the same.

MASTER. His hands? Oh yes. Dirty, you think?

FYODOR. He's a peasant, isn't he? And there'll be ladies here.

MASTER. All right, then.

FYODOR. And another thing I was going to tell you: the coachman came in yesterday to complain he couldn't keep his place clean on account of the dogs.

MASTER (*absent-mindedly*). Dogs? What dogs?

FYODOR. They brought three borzois for the young master, and they put them in the coach-house.

MASTER (*irritated*). Tell my wife. See what she thinks. I haven't the time for this kind of thing now.

FYODOR. But you know how partial she is . . .

MASTER. Well, whatever she thinks, she'll get her way. All *I* get from that boy is trouble. Anyway, I've no time now.

Enter TANYA *with* SEMYON. *He is wearing a* poddyovka *— a light, tight-fitting coat — and he is smiling.*

SEMYON. You wanted me in here?

MASTER. Yes, yes. Show me your hands . . . All right. Fine. Splendid. Now listen, my friend. When we go in there I want you to do just what you did before — I want you to sit down snd surrender yourself to sensation. Don't think about anything.

SEMYON. What would I be wanting to think for? Thinking don't help.

MASTER. Quite, quite, quite. The less conscious you are, the more powerful it will be. Don't think. Just do as the mood takes you. If you want to sleep — sleep. If you want to get up and walk about — then get up and walk about. Do you understand?

SEMYON. Certainly I understand. There's nothing complicated about that.

MASTER. The main thing is not to feel self-conscious. Because you may get one or two surprises yourself. What you have to realise is that just as we are alive, so there is an invisible world of spirits dwelling here, too.

FYODOR (*translates*). Things you can't see. Do you understand?

SEMYON (*laughs*). Of course I understand. Just like you said, it's very simple.

MASTER. You may rise up in the air, or something like that, but don't be frightened.

SEMYON. Why should I be frightened? I can do all that.

MASTER. Well, then, if we're all ready, I'll go and summon the others. What about the slates, to write on?

FYODOR. They're in my room, with the abacus. I'll go and fetch them. (*Exit* FYODOR *into the pantry.*)

MASTER. There we are, then. So don't you be self-conscious. Be more at ease.

SEMYON. Might be an idea if I took this coat off. Be more at ease like that.

MASTER. Take your coat off? No, no, that won't be necessary. (*Exit the* MASTER *up the stairs.*)

TANYA. Have you got the matches? Come on — stick them to your fingers like I showed you. And I've brought some thread. (*Laughs.*)

SEMYON (*sticks the matches to his fingers*). Thread? What do you want that for?

> Enter BETSY *at the top of the stairs. She begins to descend, but stops at the sight of* SEMYON *and* TANYA.

TANYA. I'm going to fix it from the lamp-bracket. Then as soon as they turn out the lights, I'm going to creep out from under the sofa, and I'm going to start knocking, and throwing things

about, and dangling the thread round their hair. Now, can you
remember everything?

SEMYON (*counting on his fingers*). First of all to wet the
matches, so the phosphorus glows, and then wave my arms
about — that's one. Make my teeth chatter, like so . . . two.
And the third thing I've forgotten.

TANYA. The third thing's the most important of all. Now try
and remember: when the paper lands on the table —

BETSY. Tanya! So it's you all the time! Was it you before? It
was, wasn't it! It was you!

TANYA. Oh, Miss Betsy, please, Miss Betsy, you've always been
very kind to me . . .

BETSY (*delighted*). Oh, but that's wonderful! I certainly never
thought of that!

TANYA. Please, Miss Betsy, you won't give me away?

BETSY. Not for the world!

TANYA. I was only larking about before, but now I've got something serious in mind.

BETSY. What? What is it?

TANYA. Well, you remember the peasants came and tried to buy
that land, and your Papa wouldn't sell it to them, and gave
them their paper back? Fyodor says it was the spirits that
told him not to. And then it just came into my head.

BETSY. Oh, what a clever thing you are! But how will you do it?

TANYA. Well, what I thought was, after I've done all my tricks,
I'll take out the paper about the land — I've got it here, look —
and throw it on the table. (*To* SEMYON.) Then you straightway go like this with your hands. Stretch them out, wide, wide,
lay hold of whoever's sitting next to you. (*To* BETSY.) And
as soon as he's got a hold, he'll start to squeeze. (*To* SEMYON.)
Lady or gentleman — it doesn't matter. (*To* BETSY.) Only
not your Papa — he'd never dare. (*To* SEMYON.) Just squeeze,
and keep on squeezing, and don't let go, as if you was doing
it in your sleep. Grind your teeth, or growl, like this . . .
(*To* BETSY.) And he'll go on squeezing until your Papa signs.

BETSY. Oh, but that's perfect!

TANYA (*To* SEMYON). Then when I start playing on the guitar,
you go as if you're waking up and stretching. Will you

remember all that?

SEMYON. I'll remember it all. The only trouble is, it's so funny.

Enter GRIGORY, from the pantry. He stops, unobserved, and watches them.

TANYA. Don't you go laughing, now! And don't you really go off to sleep!

SEMYON. Don't worry — I'll keep pinching my ears.

BETSY. Come on — I'll help you fix the thread.

Exit BETSY into the study.

TANYA (*to* SEMYON). Take care, then, love. Just do everything like I said, and don't be afraid. He'll sign the paper, you'll see.

Enter, at the top of the stairs, the MASTER, the PROFESSOR, SAKHATOV, the STOUT LADY, and GROSSMANN — together with the MISTRESS, the DOCTOR, VASILY, PETRISHCHEV, and MARYA. The whole party comes down the stairs, talking excitedly. Exit TANYA into the MASTER's study.

MASTER. Very well, then, very well. But please, if I may say just one thing . . .

STOUT LADY (*looking at SEMYON*). Is this the boy? *Mais il est très bien.*

MISTRESS. Very respectable-looking for a pantry-boy, yes. But when it comes to this kind of thing . . .

SAKHATOV. Wives never believe in their husbands' enterprises. You don't accept it at all?

MISTRESS. Of course not. There's something special about Kapchich, it's true, but heaven knows what all this is about.

MASTER (*stops the whole party outside his study*). If I may say just one thing before we go in . . .

STOUT LADY. Of course, but I must just say first how pleased I am that a simple peasant has turned out to be a medium. I have always said that the Westernisers were wrong and the Slavophiles were right . . .

MASTER. May I . . . ?

STOUT LADY . . . but as I always used to say to my husband,

one can overdo things. The golden mean, the golden mean. So
how is it possible to maintain that everything connected with
the common people is good, when I have seen with my own eyes . . .

MASTER. Please!

STOUT LADY. . . . . a boy only so high drinking already? I gave
him a real talking to. Afterwards he was grateful for it.

MASTER. Please, remember one thing. It is exactly the same with
this medium today as with Kapchich or any other medium —
you must not count on anything in advance. We may have a
complete materialisation, or we may have a failure.

SAKHATOV. A materialisation, even?

MISTRESS. You're surely not staying for this nonsense, are you,
doctor?

DOCTOR. Yes, I must take a look, if only once, to find out what
it is that the Professor sees in all this. To reject without proof
is also wrong.

Enter BETSY *from the study, unnoticed.*

MISTRESS. *Messieurs et mesdames,* when you have finished in
here, do please come and see me again to recover from your
emotion, and also to finish the game of cards.

STOUT LADY. Of course.

SAKHATOV. Without fail.

Exit the MISTRESS *upstairs.*

BETSY (*to* PETRISHCHEV). I should stay, if I were you. I think
I can promise you something quite out of the ordinary. Would
you like to make a bet on it?

SAKHATOV (*to the* MASTER). A materialisation, you said. What
sort of materialisation?

MASTER. The sort where a dead person comes before you. Your
father, say, or your grandfather. They take you by the hand,
perhaps, and give you something. Or someone will suddenly
rise into the air, as happened the last time the Professor and I
were present.

PROFESSOR. Of course, of course. But the main thing is the
explication of the phenomena and their subsumption under
general laws.

STOUT LADY. Yes, but what you must never forget is that these people are children, and children, as I've always said, need not only love but firmness, too.

> *Exeunt* OMNES *into the* MASTER'*s study.*
> *Except* GRIGORY, *who crosses to the study door and applies his eye to the keyhole.*
>
> *Curtain.*

Act Four

The MASTER's *study.*

The MASTER, SEMYON, GROSSMANN, *the* PROFESSOR, *the* DOCTOR, SAKHATOV, *the* STOUT LADY, BETSY, MARYA, VASILY *and* PETRISHCHEV.

MASTER. Welcome, all ye of little faith! In spite of our having a new medium, and one we found only by chance, I am hoping for some very significant manifestations.

MARYA (*to* BETSY). Do you really believe in it?

BETSY. I do today.

MARYA (*to* PETRISHCHEV). Do you believe in it?

PETRISHCHEV (*sings*). 'Can I believe those faithless vows . . . ?' (*Indicating* BETSY.) But if *she* tells me to believe in it . . .

MASTER. So are we all staying for the seance?

VASILY (*to* MARYA). We're going to stay, aren't we? Perhaps I'll think of some little surprise to do, what?

MARYA. No, don't you make me laugh. Honestly, I shan't be able to stop myself.

VASILY (*loudly*). I — shall remain — at my post.

MASTER. I would just ask those who do choose to stay not to make this the occasion for jokes. This is a serious matter.

PETRISHCHEV (*to* VASILY). Do you hear that? All right, then, so we'll stay. Vovo, sit here, and try not to be too frightened.

BETSY. Yes, you can laugh. But wait till you see what happens.

VASILY. Why? What *is* going to happen? There's going to be some kind of trick, what?

PETRISHCHEV (*trembles*). Oh dear, I'm frightened! I'm frightened, Miss Marya! Look, my trees are all of a knemble!

BETSY (*laughs*). That's quite enough from you.

MASTER. Sit down. Sit down.

They sit.

STOUT LADY. Nowadays young people deny everything.

VASILY. What? I never deny myself anything!

STOUT LADY. But how can the supernatural possibly be denied? People say it's contrary to reason. But if reason itself is unreasonable, then what? When you think that every evening right here in Moscow, on the Sadovaya — have you heard about this? — things have been seen . . . My husband's brother — what do you call that? *Mon beau-frère* — I can only think of it in French — I can't remember any of these names except in French . . . Anyway, he went along to the Sadovaya three nights running and saw absolutely nothing at all.

MASTER. Sit down, Semyon.

SEMYON. Very good, sir. (*Sits down on the edge of the chair.*)

MASTER. Sit properly, now.

PROFESSOR. Properly back in the chair. And perfectly at ease. (*Arranges* SEMYON *on the chair.*)

> The YOUNG PEOPLE *laugh.*

MASTER (*raising his voice*). I must ask those who have elected to stay not to play the fool, and to treat the matter seriously. Otherwise there could be serious consequences. Vovo, are you listening? Either go away, or sit still and pay attention.

VASILY. Attention? All right, then. Atten-*shun!* (*Hides behind the* STOUT LADY'*s back.*)

MASTER. Professor, will you put him into the trance?

PROFESSOR. Why ask me, when we have Mr. Grossmann here? He has both much more practice and much more power. Mr. Grossmann!

GROSSMANN. Gentlemen, I am not strictly speaking a spiritualist. I have merely studied hypnosis. Hypnosis I have studied in all its known manifestations, it is true. But what people call spiritualism is something about which I know absolutely nothing. From putting the subject into a trance I may expect the phenomena of hypnosis with which I am familiar: lethargy, loss of willpower, anaesthesia, analgesia, catalepsy, and every type of suggestibility. Here, however, it is not these but other phenomena that are being proposed for investigation, and it would therefore be desirable to know of what type these anticipated phenomena are, and what scientific significance they possess.

SAKHATOV. I fully concur in Mr. Grossmann's opinion. Such an explanation would be of the greatest interest.

MASTER. Professor, I am sure you will not refuse us a short word of explanation.

PROFESSOR. Certainly, I can oblige, if that would seem desirable. (*To the* DOCTOR.) If you would be kind enough to take his temperature and pulse. My explanation will of necessity be superficial and brief.

MASTER. Yes, just a short word.

DOCTOR (*administers the thermometer*). Here we are, then, young fellow-me-lad.

SEMYON. Sir.

PROFESSOR (*rises, turns to the* STOUT LADY, *and then sits down again*). Ladies and gentlemen. Until recently we knew of only four forms of convertible energy. We knew of dynamic energy, thermal, electrical, and chemical energy. But these four forms of energy are a long way from exhausting all the variety of its manifestations. The forms in which energy manifests itself are many, and one of these new, little-known forms is what we are investigating here tonight. I am speaking of psychic energy.

> *Whispers and giggles in the* YOUNG PEOPLE's *corner. The* PROFESSOR *stops, looks round sternly, and then continues.*

Psychic energy has been known to mankind for a very long time indeed. Predictions, premonitions, clairvoyance, and many other things — these are all nothing but manifestations of psychic energy. The phenomena produced by it have long been familiar. But the energy itself was not identified as such until very recently, not until it was possible to identify the material in which the vibrations occur that give rise to psychic energy. And precisely as the phenomenon of light was inexplicable until the existence of a weightless substance, the ether, was recognised, so psychic phenomena seemed mysterious until it was discovered, as is now established

beyond any doubt, that in the interstices between the particles
of ether there is another weightless substance, more rarefied
even than the ether itself, which is not subject to the laws of
the three-dimensional world . . .

More whispers, giggles, and squeaks. The PROFESSOR
again looks sternly round.

And exactly as mathematical calculations have irrefutably
established the existence of the weightless ether, which gives
us the phenomena of light and electricity, so a brilliant series
of the most precise experiments by two men of genius,
Hermann Schmidt and Josef Schmatzoven, have confirmed
beyond doubt the existence of this other substance that fills
the universe, and that might be termed spiritual ether.

STOUT LADY. Ah yes, now I understand. I am most grateful.

PROFESSOR. And so a whole series of strictly scientific
experiments and investigations, as I had the honour to inform
you, have made clear to us the laws governing psychic
phenomena . . .

MASTER. Professor, couldn't you . . . shorten this a little?

PROFESSOR (*ignores him*). These experiments have made it
clear to us that the immersion of certain persons in a hypnotic
state — a state distinguished from normal sleep only by the
fact that upon immersion physiological activity is not only not
reduced but is in fact always increased, as we recently observed
— that the immersion of any subject in this state inevitably
brings in its train certain disturbances of the spiritual ether —
disturbances precisely like those produced by the immersion of
a solid body in liquid. These disturbances are what we term
psychic phenomena.

SAKHATOV. This is all entirely reasonable and comprehensible.
But may I ask one question? If, as you were kind enough to
explain, the immersion of the medium in a trance produces
disturbances of the spiritual ether, why do these disturbances
always find expression — as is usually assumed at spiritualist
seances — in the manifestation of activity by the spirits of the
dead?

PROFESSOR. Simply because the particles of this spiritual ether are nothing other than the spirits of the living, the dead, and the unborn; so that any agitation of the spiritual ether inevitably produces a certain movement of the particles in it. And this movement of the particles is purely and simply the spirits entering into communication with each other.

STOUT LADY (*to* SAKHATOV). What's difficult to understand about that? It's all so simple . . . Thank you very much indeed.

MASTER. I think, if everything is clear now, we might proceed.

DOCTOR. This young fellow is in a completely normal state: temperature 98.9, pulse 74.

PROFESSOR (*takes out his notebook and writes*). Confirmation of what I've just told you may be found in this fact: that the immersion of the medium in a trance, as we shall shortly be seeing, inevitably produces a rise in temperature and pulse, exactly as in hypnosis.

MASTER. Yes, yes. Forgive me, but I did just wish to say one word to our friend here in answer to his question about how we know that it is the spirits of the dead who are communicating with us. We know because the spirit who comes before us speaks to us directly — speaks to us as simply as I am speaking to you now — and tells us who he is, how he is, where he is, and why he has come. At the last seance it was a Spaniard, Don Castilios, and he told us everything. He told us who he was and when he had died, and he said that it went hard for him because he had taken part in the Inquisition. Moreover he told us what was happening to him at the precise moment he was talking to us. And what was happening was that he was due to be born again on earth, so that he was in fact unable to finish the conversation he had begun with us. But you'll see for yourself . . .

STOUT LADY. Oh, how fascinating! Perhaps he was born in a house in our country, and he's a little baby somewhere now.

MASTER. Very possibly.

PROFESSOR. I think it is time we began.

MASTER. I merely wanted to say . . .

PROFESSOR. Time is getting on.

MASTER. Oh, very well, then. So let us proceed. Mr Grossmann, would you be good enough to put the medium into a trance?

GROSSMANN. How would you prefer me to do it? There are a number of ways in use. There is Braid's method. There is the Egyptian symbol. There is Charcot's method.

MASTER (*to the* PROFESSOR). It makes no odds, I think?

PROFESSOR. Quite immaterial.

GROSSMANN. Then I shall use my own method, the one that I demonstrated in Odessa.

MASTER. Please.

> GROSSMANN *waves his hands over* SEMYON, *who closes his eyes and stretches.*

GROSSMANN. He is going to sleep . . . he is going to sleep . . . he's gone. A remarkably rapid onset of hypnosis. He seems to have passed already into the anaesthetic state. He is a quite unusually receptive subject, and we could perform a number of rather interesting experiments. We could start off by sticking pins into his hands. If you so desire.

PROFESSOR (*to* MASTER). Do you notice how the medium's trance is affecting Grossmann? He is beginning to vibrate.

MASTER. Yes, yes. May we now extinguish the lights?

SAKHATOV. But why is darkness necessary?

PROFESSOR. Darkness? Why, because darkness is one of the conditions in which psychic energy manifests itself, just as a given temperature is a condition of certain manifestations of chemical or dynamic energy.

MASTER. And indeed it is not always necessary. Many people, myself among them, have seen manifestations both by candlelight and in full sunlight.

PROFESSOR. May we extinguish the lights?

MASTER. Yes, yes. (*Extinguishes the candles.*) Ladies and gentlemen! May I now please have your attention?

PETRISHCHEV. I liked the sound of that Spanish fellow. The way he dived off head first in the middle of the conversation, to go and get himself born.

BETSY. Just you wait and see what's going to happen this time!

PETRISHCHEV. The only thing I'm frightened of is that Vovo will do his piglet imitation.

VASILY. Oh, would you like me to? I'll try to oblige . . .

MASTER. Ladies and gentlemen, if you please, I must ask you not to talk.

Silence. SEMYON's *phosphorescent hands move about in the darkness.*

A light! Do you see the light?
SAKHATOV. A light! Yes, yes, I do. But if I may say so . . .
STOUT LADY. Where, where? Oh, I never saw it! There it is! Oh!

Crash.

What's that?
PROFESSOR. That's Grossmann.
MASTER. He keeps moving about.
PROFESSOR. He is vibrating. A double power.

The light appears again.

MASTER. That light. That's *him,* isn't it?
SAKHATOV. Who?
MASTER. Nikolai the Greek. That's his light. Isn't that so, Professor?
SAKHATOV. Who or what is Nikolai the Greek?
PROFESSOR. A certain Greek who was a monk in Constantinople during the reign of Constantine. He visited us on the last occasion.
STOUT LADY. Where is he? Where is he? I can't see him!
MASTER. You are not supposed to see him yet. Professor, he is always particularly well disposed towards you. Question him.
PROFESSOR (*in a special voice*). Nikolai! Is it you?

Two knocks.

MASTER. It's him! It's him!
STOUT LADY. Ai ai! I'm going!
SAKHATOV. Why are we to suppose that it's him?
MASTER. Because there were two knocks. Two knocks are the affirmative reply. Otherwise there would have been silence.

Silence. Repressed giggling in the YOUNG PEOPLE's *corner. A sound.*

DOCTOR. Something then.
MASTER. Fell on the table.
STOUT LADY. What? What?
MASTER. A pencil. Professor, a pencil!
PROFESSOR. Good, good.

Another sound.

STOUT LADY. Now what?
MASTER. Penwiper.
SAKHATOV. Penwiper?
MASTER. Transported itself from the desk to the table.
PROFESSOR. Good. I am keeping a check on Grossmann, as
    well as the medium.

Crash.

STOUT LADY. Ai ai ai!
MASTER. The lampshade.
SAKHATOV. If I may be permitted, I should like to look and
    see whether this is all being done by the medium himself.
MASTER. You think so? Then sit next to him and hold his hands.
    He is asleep, though, you may be sure of that.
SAKHATOV. I'll change places . . . A-a-a-a-h! Something . . . in
    the air! Touched my head! That's odd.

SEMYON *growls.*

PROFESSOR. You hear that? Something is growling through the
    medium. That is the effect of Grossmann's presence. A new
    phenomenon. I must note it down.

*The PROFESSOR opens the door, and holds his notebook
in the light.*

MASTER. Yes, but we mustn't leave Nikolai without an answer.
GROSSMANN. The subject is in full hypnosis. It would be rather
    interesting now to induce cataleptic rigidity.
PROFESSOR. Listen to Grossmann! I told you.
GROSSMANN. If you wish, I could . . .
DOCTOR. If I were you, old chap, I think I'd let the Professor
    run things. This is turning out to be a rather serious business.

PROFESSOR. Leave him. He is speaking in a trance now.

The PROFESSOR *closes the door.*

STOUT LADY. Oh, I *am* pleased I decided to be here! It's frightening, but all the same I'm terribly pleased, because I always used to say to my husband . . .

MASTER. I must ask you to be quiet.

STOUT LADY. I was merely going to say that as I used to say to my husband. . . Ai!

MASTER. What? What?

STOUT LADY. He touched my hair! Something touched my hair. He seized me by the hair!

MASTER (*in a whisper*). Don't be afraid. It's all right. Give him your hand. Their hands are usually cold, but I love that.

STOUT LADY. I *won't* give him my hand! Not for anything in the world!

MASTER. He is here, and he is seeking communication. Who wants to ask him anything?

SAKHATOV. I will, if I may.

PROFESSOR. Minister — please.

SAKHATOV. Do I believe in all this or do I not?

Two knocks.

PROFESSOR. Affirmative.

SAKHATOV. I shall ask another question, if I may. Do I, or do I not, have a ten-rouble note in my pocket?

A fusillade of knocking.

PROFESSOR. I would ask everyone present to desist from vague questions, or questions of a humorous nature. He doesn't like it.

SAKHATOV. Ah! Something touched my head again . . . What's this? I seem to have got hold of a piece of thread.

MASTER. A piece of thread? Hold on to it, then. That often happens. Not only thread, but silken cords — sometimes of the greatest antiquity.

SAKHATOV. Yes, but where did the thread come from . . . ? Uh! If I may say so, I have just been struck upon the head by

something large and soft. May we have some light? I think
it's . . . Is it a cushion . . . ?

PROFESSOR. Please don't disturb the manifestation.

STOUT LADY. No, for heaven's sake, don't disturb it! I should
like to ask a question as well. Is that permissible?

MASTER. Yes, yes. Ask away.

STOUT LADY. It's about my stomach. Is that allowed? I want
to ask which I should take for it — aconite or belladonna?

Silence, then suddenly VASILY *makes a noise like a baby
crying.*

What?

PROFESSOR. A baby, by the sound of it.

STOUT LADY. Then it's true! It's true! This one's been born
again as well!

MASTER. Vovo! I get nothing out of that boy but idiocy! Vovo,
if you can't behave properly, get out!

VASILY. Oh, right, then.

Exeunt VASILY, PETRISHCHEV, BETSY *and* MARYA,
their hands to their mouths, snorting with laughter.

STOUT LADY. Oh, what a pity! We can't ask him anything, now
he's been born.

MASTER. He hasn't been born at all. That was just Vovo's
nonsense. *He* is here. You may go on questioning him.

PROFESSOR. This often happens. Jokes and gibes — they are
the commonest phenomena of all upon these occasions. I
submit that he is still here. We can in any case ask. Would you
like to oblige?

MASTER. No, please — you do it. My mood has been completely
destroyed. So unpleasant. So tactless.

PROFESSOR. Very well, then. Nikolai! Are you still here?

Two knocks. The bell is rung. SEMYON *growls.*

SAKHATOV. Uh! I'm being . . . squeezed! It's the medium! He's
taken hold of my arm!

PROFESSOR. He's taken hold of mine, as well. But this
manifestation is entirely unexpected! An influence upon the

medium himself! But this has never happened before. Can you find out what Grossmann is doing? This is where we need our fullest attention. It is rather difficult for me, since l am being squeezed.

A noise.

MASTER. Something has fallen on the table.
PROFESSOR. What? What?
MASTER. Paper! A folded sheet of paper!

Another noise.

What's this? An inkwell . . . and a pen!

SEMYON *growls.*

PROFESSOR. But this is an entirely novel manifestation! Not psychic energy called forth by the medium, but the medium himself. Open the inkwell and put the pen on the paper. I believe he will write.

Silence.

MASTER. The pen is still not writing. The paper is still folded.
PROFESSOR. Look and see what sort of paper it is. Quickly now. The disturbances are plainly being produced by a double power — by him and Grossmann together.
MASTER (*opens the door and examines the paper*). How extraordinary! This paper is the agreement with the peasants that I refused to sign yesterday and gave back to them. Conceivably *he* wants me to sign it now, do you think?
PROFESSOR. Of course! Of course! Ask him.
MASTER. Nikolai! Do you or do you not wish me . . . ?

Two knocks.

PROFESSOR. Obviously he does.

The MASTER *signs the paper. There is the sound of the guitar and the accordion being played.* SEMYON *stretches and clears his throat.*

MASTER. The medium is waking up. We can light the candles.

PROFESSOR. Doctor — temperature and pulse, if you would.
You will see that we find a rise in both.

MASTER (*lights the candles*). How now, all ye ladies and
gentlemen of little faith?

DOCTOR (*administering the thermometer to* SEMYON). Well,
then, young fellow. Had a little snooze, have we? Pop this in,
then, and let's just feel your wrist.

SAKHATOV (*shrugs*). I can certainly confirm that the medium
could not have done everything that occurred. But the thread?
I should like an explanation of the thread.

MASTER. The thread, the thread! We had phenomena that
deserve to be taken a little more seriously than that.

SAKHATOV. Well, I don't know. At all events, *je réserve mon
opinion*.

STOUT LADY. How can you possibly say you reserve
judgment? What about the little cherub with the wings? You
must have seen that! I thought for a moment I was seeing
things. But then it became as clear as day — you'd have thought
it was alive.

SAKHATOV. I can speak only about what I saw. I saw no cherub.

STOUT LADY. What? It was absolutely clearly visible! The monk
was to the left of it, all garbed in black and bending over it!

SAKHATOV. Ridiculous exaggeration.

STOUT LADY. Doctor, you must have seen it. It rose up from
your side of the table.

The DOCTOR *continues to measure* SEMYON's *pulse.*

(*To* GROSSMANN:) And the light! The light that was
emanating from him! Particularly from around his dear little
face. And his expression was so meek and gentle — there was
something of heaven in it. (*Smiles tenderly to herself.*)

GROSSMANN. I saw a phosphorescence, and objects moving
from place to place. I saw nothing more.

STOUT LADY. Oh, come, come! That's just you. That's just
because you belong to the school of Charcot, and you don't
believe in a life beyond the grave. But no one now, no one in
the world, will ever make me stop believing in a future life.

GROSSMANN *moves away from her.*

No, no, say what you like — this is one of the happiest
moments of my life. The other was when I heard Sarasate play
the violin — and now this . . . Tell me, my friend — what did
you feel? Was it difficult for you?

SEMYON (*laughs*). It certainly was!

STOUT LADY. But nonetheless you managed to bear it?

SEMYON. I certainly did! (*To the* MASTER:) May I go now?

MASTER. Yes, yes. Off you go.

Exit SEMYON.

DOCTOR. His pulse is unchanged, and his temperature has gone
down somewhat.

PROFESSOR. Gone down? (*Reflects, and then suddenly sees
it*). And that of course is exactly what it should have done!
There had to be a fall in temperature! The two fields of energy
must have intersected each other, and produced something in
the form of interference. Of course. Of course.

MASTER. My only regret is that there was not a full
materialisation. All the same . . . Ladies and gentlemen, please
— let us adjourn to the sitting-room.

He ushers the others out, all talking at once.

STOUT LADY. What particularly struck me was when he
fluttered his little wings, and you could see him rise up in the
air . . .

GROSSMANN. If we had confined ourselves to hypnosis alone,
we could have had a complete success — we could have
produced total epilepsy . . .

SAKHATOV. Interesting; but not entirely convincing. That is
all I can say . . .

The MASTER *remains alone with the paper. Enter*
FYODOR.

MASTER. Well, Fyodor, what a seance it was. Astonishing. It
turns out that we have to let the peasants have that land on
their own terms.

FYODOR. Does it, indeed!

MASTER. What else could I do? Just imagine — this paper that I gave back to them turned up on the table. So I signed.

FYODOR. However did it get there?

MASTER. I don't know, but get there it certainly did. If only
the peasants were still here they could have it.

FYODOR. I think I might be able to find them.

MASTER. Could you give it to them? (*Hands him the paper.*)
They seemed quite keen to have it. Tell them I reflected a little
further on the matter.

> *Exeunt the* MASTER *and* FYODOR. TANYA, *alone in
> the room, crawls out from under the sofa and laughs.*

TANYA. But my heavens, I got a scare when he took hold of the
thread! (*Squeals.*) Never mind — it worked! He signed!

> *Enter* GRIGORY.

GRIGORY. So it was you, was it?

TANYA. What was me?

GRIGORY. Making fools of them all.

TANYA. What's that got to do with you?

GRIGORY. Well, you don't think the mistress is going to give
you a pat on the back for this, do you? No, you've had your
fun and games, and now you're for it. I'll tell her all about
your little tricks, if you don't do things the way I want.

TANYA. I shan't! And you shan't do anything to me, either!

> *Enter* FYODOR.

FYODOR (*to* TANYA). How did you get in here?

GRIGORY. That'd be telling!

FYODOR (*to* TANYA). Here, take the peasants their paper. He's
signed it after all.

GRIGORY. Heavens above, she says, has he now?

> *Enter* YAKOV, *his hands full of cutlery.*

Look at him! He's come into the Master's study to clean the
silver! Think you'll be safe from her in here, do you? (*To*
TANYA:) All right, then. You've got a little job to do. And
now you've got me to help you.

Exeunt TANYA *and* GRIGORY.

YAKOV. It's a living shame! She's going to turn me off! You! She says. You're always breaking things! You forgot about Fifka! You went and let the peasants into the kitchen against my express orders! But you can tell her — I didn't know anything about that! It was just Tanya said: 'Take them into the kitchen.' I didn't know whose orders it was or wasn't.

FYODOR. Did she really say you was to be turned off?

YAKOV. Just this minute! You'll stand up for me, won't you? There's my family just begun to set themselves to rights. Now I lose my place and down we go again. Please stand up for me.

Enter the MISTRESS.

MISTRESS (*to* YAKOV). *Now* what are you doing? Are you going to lay the supper in here? Or are you merely stealing all the household belongings that you haven't managed to break?

FYODOR. I wonder if I might have a quiet word with you about Yakov here?

MISTRESS. A quiet word? What quiet word?

Enter GRIGORY, *dishevelled and excited, with* SEMYON *after him.*

GRIGORY. He's trying to kill me!

SEMYON. I'm telling you, now — stop pestering her!

GRIGORY. I'll teach you how to fight! You rural oaf! You murderous bumpkin!

MISTRESS. What *is* this? Where do you think you are — in a taproom?

GRIGORY. I can't live with this lump of a peasant around!

MISTRESS. Have you taken leave of your senses?

GRIGORY. I may be a footman, but I've got my pride, and I'm not going to let any peasant go shoving at me.

MISTRESS. But what happened?

GRIGORY. This Semyon of yours — he's suddenly come over all brave, now he's been sitting with his betters. He's started fighting.

MISTRESS. Why? What about?

GRIGORY. Lord knows.

MISTRESS (*to* SEMYON). What does this mean?

SEMYON. Why does he keep pestering her?

MISTRESS. What has been going on down there?

SEMYON (*smiling*). What's been going on is that he keeps grabbing at Tanya, and she don't want him. So I pushed him away with my hand . . . Like that, just a little push.

GRIGORY. He pushed me away all right! He almost broke my ribs! He tore my coat! And you know what he says? He says: 'That power I had just now — I can feel it coming on me again!' And he begins to squeeze me . . .

MISTRESS (*to* SEMYON). How dare you fight in my house!

FYODOR. If I might explain, Ma'am — Semyon here has feelings towards Tanya. Indeed they're engaged to be married. Whereas Gigrory — well, the truth has to be told — he don't behave rightly and decently with the girl. So then I suppose Semyon here took umbrage.

GRIGORY. It wasn't so. It was out of malice, because I found out about their swindling.

MISTRESS. What swindling?

GRIGORY. At the seance. All those tricks — that wasn't Semyon, that was Tanya. I saw her with my own eyes, creeping out from under the sofa.

MISTRESS. Creeping out from under the sofa? What is all this?

GRIGORY. I'll take my oath on it. And she brought the paper with her, and threw it down on the table. If it hadn't been for her, the paper wouldn't never have been signed, and the land wouldn't never have been sold to the peasants.

MISTRESS. You saw this with your own eyes?

GRIGORY. With my own eyes. Have her called. She'll never deny it.

MISTRESS. Call her.

Noises off.

DOORKEEPER (*off*). You can't go in there! You can't go in there!

The DOORKEEPER *appears. The* THREE PEASANTS

force their way past him, the 2ND PEASANT *in the lead. The* 3RD PEASANT *stumbles, falls over, and holds his nose.*

No! Out! You can't come in here!

Exit GRIGORY.

2ND PEASANT. What's the matter? You don't think we're after doing something wrong, do you? We want to pay the money!

1ST PEASANT. Indeed, now he's put his hand to it and signed, the business is settled. All we want to do is to furnish up the money with our thanks.

MISTRESS. Wait just one moment before you start thanking anyone. It was all a trick. It's not settled yet by any means. It's not sold yet at all.

Enter the MASTER.

MASTER (*at the sight of the* MISTRESS *and all the rest of them*). Oh. You're in here, are you? Well, I'll just . . . (*Starts to go out again.*)

MISTRESS. No, no! You come in, if you please! I kept telling you. You mustn't sell that land on credit, I said. Everyone kept telling you. And you let them pull the wool over your eyes and treat you like a complete fool.

MASTER. Pull the wool over my eyes? How? I don't understand.

MISTRESS. You should be ashamed of yourself! Here you are, an old man with grey hair, and they make a fool of you and laugh at you as if you were a little child. You begrudge your son a miserable three hundred roubles to keep up his position in society, and all the time like a complete idiot you're being taken for thousands!

MASTER. Now calm down, my dear.

1ST PEASANT. We only want to receive over the money to you . . .

3RD PEASANT (*gets the money out*). Then give us leave to depart, for the love of Christ!

MISTRESS. Wait, wait.

Enter GRIGORY *and* TANYA.

(*to* TANYA). Were you in this room while the seance was taking place?

> TANYA *sighs, and looks round at* FYODOR, SEMYON *and the* MASTER.

GRIGORY. It's no good trying to wriggle out of it, when I saw you with my own eyes.

MISTRESS. Answer me: were you? You might as well own up, because I know everything. I shan't do anything to you. *He's* the one who's in the dock. Your master. Did you throw the paper down on to the table?

TANYA. I don't know what to answer. Just — won't you let me go home?

MISTRESS (*to the* MASTER). You see? They're making a fool of you.

> *Enter* BETSY, *unnoticed.*

TANYA. Let me go, Ma'am!

MISTRESS. No, my dear! You may have cost us several thousand roubles. Land has been sold that needn't have been sold.

TANYA. Let me go!

MISTRESS. No, you are going to answer for this. We can't have swindling. I am going to hand you over to the courts.

BETSY (*stepping forward*). Let her go, Mama. If you want to bring charges against her, then you must bring them against both of us, because we did it together.

MISTRESS. Oh, well, if you were in it, then of course nothing was to be expected but black mischief.

> *Enter the* PROFESSOR.

PROFESSOR (*to the* MASTER). Ah, here you are. No, as I was saying, you must read this report on the Thirteenth Spiritualist Congress in Chicago. There is a remarkable speech by Schmidt.

MASTER. Ah. Most interesting.

MISTRESS. I'm going to tell you something much more interesting still. It turns out that you and my husband have both been made fools of by this little hussy. Betsy is trying to take it on herself, but that's just to irritate me. You've been made fools of by an illiterate young girl. And you believe it! All your psychic phenomena — there weren't any! They were all done by her!

PROFESSOR. How do you mean?

MISTRESS. I mean that it was she who played the guitar in the dark, and did all the rest of your nonsense, because she has just owned up.

PROFESSOR (*smiling*). So what does this prove?

MISTRESS. It proves that all your psychic business is rubbish! That's what it proves!

PROFESSOR. From the fact that this girl tried to deceive us it follows that all our psychic business, as you choose to call it, is nonsense? (*Smiles.*) What an extraordinary conclusion! It may very well be that this girl tried to deceive us; that often happens. It may be that she did in fact do some of the things. But what she did was done by her; and what was a manifestation of psychic energy was a manifestation of psychic energy. It is even highly probable that this girl's activities touched off — as one might say, *elicited* — the manifestation of psychic energy, and gave it its particular form.

MISTRESS. Another lecture!

PROFESSOR (*sternly*). You tell us, my dear lady, that this girl and this charming young lady here may possibly have done some of the things. But the light that we all saw — but the fall in temperature in the first instance and the rise in temperature in the second — but Grossmann's excitement and vibration — what then, did the girl do all this as well? But these are facts! Facts, my dear lady! No, there are some things that have to be investigated and understood before they can be talked about — things that are too serious, much too serious . . .

MASTER. And the child that Marya Vasılyevna clearly saw! And indeed that I saw! That couldn't have been done by this girl.

MISTRESS. You think you're clever, don't you? But you're a fool!

MASTER. Come, Professor, let us retire to my study . . . Or rather, let us retire out of my study.

PROFESSOR (*shrugging his shoulders*). Yes, how remote we are from Europe still.

Exeunt the MASTER *and the* PROFESSOR.

MISTRESS. They made an utter fool of him — and he can't see it! (*To* YAKOV:) What do you want?

YAKOV. Am I to lay for company as well as family?

MISTRESS. Are you to lay for company . . . ? What are you doing here at all? (*To* FYODOR:) Take the silver off him! (*To* YAKOV:) Out! This instant! Out! (*Indicating* YAKOV.) He's at the back of it all! He'll drive me into my grave! Yesterday he almost starved the dog to death! A creature that had never done him the slightest harm! As if that weren't enough, he then brought infectious peasants into the kitchen! And now here they are again. He's at the back of it all! Out! Out! Out! You're dismissed! You're discharged! (*To* SEMYON:) And if you ever dare to make a row in my house again I shall teach you a lesson you won't forget! You horrible peasant!

2ND PEASANT. Well, then, if he's a horrible peasant, there's no reason to keep him. You can give him his discharge, and there's an end to it.

MISTRESS (*inspecting the* 3RD PEASANT). And look at this one! He's got something wrong with his nose! He's diseased! He's a reservoir of infection! I kept saying yesterday not to let them in — and here they are again! Get them out of here!

FYODOR. What, then, aren't we to take their money?

MISTRESS. Their money? Yes, take their money — but get *them* out. Out! Out! Out! This instant! Especially this diseased one. He's absolutely *rotten* with infection!

3RD PEASANT. You're wrong there, mother. Indeed you are. You ask anyone. You ask my old woman. I'm as sound as a flute.

MISTRESS. Is he still debating the point? Out! Out! They all do it just to spite me! I can't go on like this! I simply can't go on! Fetch the doctor!

GRIGORY. The doctor . . . (*Exit* GRIGORY.)

MISTRESS. The doctor! The doctor!

YAKOV. The doctor . . . (*Exit* YAKOV.)

MISTRESS. Doctor! Doctor! (*Exit the* MISTRESS, *sobbing.*)

TANYA. What about me, Miss Betsy? What am I to do now?

BETSY. Don't worry. Everything will be all right. You take the train with them. I'll settle everything here. (*Exit* BETSY.)

1ST PEASANT. What about it, then, mister? Can we receive out the money now?

2ND PEASANT. Take the money and let us go.

3RD PEASANT (*fumbles with the money*). If I'd have known, I'd never in my life have took it on. It withers you up worse than the wickedest illness.

FYODOR (*to the* DOORKEEPER). Take them through into my room, where the abacus is. I'll receive the money in there. Off you go now.

DOORKEEPER. This way.

FYODOR. And give thanks to Tanya. If it wasn't for her, you'd still be without the land.

1ST PEASANT. Indeed, as she proposed, so she in good earnest brought to be.

3RD PEASANT. She made men out of us. And how would it have gone with us if she hadn't? Our plots are small. Nowhere to turn out a cow, not even a hen. Fare you well, you clever lass. When you're in the village, you come and eat honey with us.

2ND PEASANT. Just let me get home, and I'll start preparing the wedding and brewing the beer. All you have to do is to come.

TANYA. I'm coming, never you fear! (*Squeals.*) Semyon! Hasn't it all just come out right?

Exeunt the PEASANTS.

FYODOR. Well, then, Tanya, God be with you. When you're living in your own little home I'll come and visit you. Will you take me in?

TANYA. We'll take you in, Fyodor, my dear. As you were my own true father, we will. (*Embraces and kisses him.*)

Curtain.